A Full Pull

A Full Pull

The Sport of Tractor Pulling

Geoff Ashcroft

FARMING PRESS

First published 1993

ISBN 0 85236 261 7

A catalogue record for this book is available from the British Library

Published by Farming Press Books
Wharfedale Road, Ipswich IP1 4LG, United Kingdom

Distributed in North America by Diamond Farm Enterprises
Box 537, Alexandria Bay, NY 13607, USA

Front cover
Dave Prince's Just Another Invader
Running Deere, driven by Alistair Broad

Back cover
The rear of the Starlight Express team coach

Frontispiece
The Whittinghams' Snoopy in action at Great Eccleston in 1992

Cover design by Andrew Thistlethwaite
Typeset by Galleon Photosetting, Ipswich
Printed and bound in Great Britain by Butler & Tanner,
Frome and London

Contents

Acknowledgements

I would like to thank everyone who helped in any way with the research and preparation of this book, particularly those who provided photographs.

My thanks to the WPI/NTPA, in particular David Shreier, the president and chief executive officer of the WPI, and Rhdawnda Bliss, editor of the NTPA's *The Puller* for information and photographs used in Chapter 1.

Thanks also to the BTPA, including all past and present members who have taken the trouble to discuss tractor pulling and supply photographs and information for which I am very grateful.

I would also like to thank Anne Jones, Tom and Mark Osborne, Mike Hansard and Nick Young, John Bowen-Jones, Peter and Stephen Clarke, Ted Corner, Stan Cookson, Paul Turnham, Mark Matthews, Trevor Pitman, Mike Lawrence, Jim Snell and Tim Turner and the Massey Lads for their help.

Thanks also to Nigel Hughes and Henry de Graaf for the use of photographs.

Introduction

Tractor pulling, the world's most powerful motor sport, has been described as a sport in which the unstoppable attempt to pull the immovable.

Tuned-up 'tractors' producing thousands of horsepower compete against one another to determine which tractor can haul a heavily ballasted sledge the greatest distance along a 100 metre track. This so-called weight transfer sledge is a weighted trailer which increases the load on the tractor as the pulled distance increases, and the distance achieved is a 'measured pull'.

The Starlight Express tractor pulling team sums it all up.

It is reported that the sport originated in the United States shortly after the turn of the twentieth century, then using horses, as neighbouring farmers slogged it out to see who had the strongest ploughing horse.

Naturally, with the introduction of technology, tractors took over from horses and by 1929, the first motorised tractor pulls were recorded in Vaughnsville, Ohio, and Bowling Green, Missouri. The object of the exercise then was to move the sledge—a flat steel pan, ballasted with stones and heavy lumps of concrete—a distance of only ten yards. There was no defined track and competitors just hooked up and pulled the sledge in any direction they could, and if the sledge moved ten yards, regardless of direction, it was classed as a full pull. This became recognised as dead-weight pulling.

However, this method was a rather crude and destructive way of testing tractor strength, as many tractors broke in half as a result of the enormous stresses imposed upon them—a far cry from the sophisticated sledges and high performance tractors seen competing in the sport today.

Following the introduction of this 'new' sport to the UK in 1977 by Tom Osborne and his son Mark from Romsey, Hampshire, the British Tractor Pullers Association (BTPA) was formed, and tractor pulling divisions with specific weight classes, rules, regulations and safety features were quickly adopted from a 'loose' translation of the rule book of the American National Tractor Pullers Association (NTPA). This was intended to give the British tractor pulling scene a rudder by which it could be steered and not left to wander aimlessly.

Currently the BTPA boasts over 50 competing tractors in five pulling divisions, the divisions being pro stock tractors, super stock tractors, two-wheel drive trucks (a slow-growing class in which there are currently only two vehicles), modified and mini modified tractors. And within each pulling division, there are specific weight classes at which tractors compete.

To win the title of British Champion, tractor pullers compete for points (with the exception of the BTPA's two-wheel drive trucks) in their specific weight classes at authorised events. And at the end of the season, top tractors are selected from each class to take part in a European championship event, which is organised annually by the European Tractor Pulling Committee (ETPC), which is a co-ordinating body with objectives to pursue and promote tractor pulling throughout Europe.

A European championship event is run over two days each year, usually during the first weekend in September, in one of the ETPC's 12 affiliated member countries. It is the premier tractor pulling event in Europe and culminates in the allocation of European Champion titles for the best tractors in Europe.

1 American Beginnings

The roots of tractor pulling have been traced to America, where 'pulls' took place not long after the turn of the twentieth century. In these early days before the advent of the tractor, a form of pulling took place with horses, as local farmers met up at weekends to settle the score on who had the strongest ploughing horse.

By 1929, tractors were starting to take the place of horses in pulling, and a growing enthusiasm for this test of strength led to the first-recorded motorised tractor pulls at Vaughnsville, Ohio, and Bowling Green, Missouri.

During the 1950s, neighbouring farmers would entertain an audience to see whose tractor had the best traction, performance and, in some cases, strength. At this time, there was no such thing as a weight transfer sledge. Instead, farmers were 'deadweight pulling', using large steel skid pans loaded with stones and concrete, nicknamed 'stoneboats'. Tractors too were occasionally used as ballast. And, as tractors were standard farm

Before the evolution of the weight transfer sledge, pullers used flat steel pans loaded with suitable ballast. In this instance, it is another tractor.

machines, competition was evenly matched. A variation on this theme was 'free for all' pulling where tractors were first ballasted to ridiculous weights, using concrete blocks and sandbags, and then hooked to the stoneboat sledge. The object was to try to creep forward over a ten-yard marker, the winner often being the only competitor with the tractor still in one piece.

It was not until the late 1950s that sledge developments started to unfold. The stoneboat sledges were too unforgiving, and pulls were too slow and over too small a distance to keep spectators interested.

The step-on sledge was a natural progression from the stoneboat sledge during the late 1950s and allowed a progressive load increase as the sledge was pulled along a track. This was quite a leap forward in sledge development and proved to be a crude forerunner to the modern-day weight transfer sledge which is currently in use throughout the world.

As its name suggests, the step-on sledge required a number of volunteers to jump onto the sledge as it was pulled along. To maintain a form of fairness for competitors pulling the step-on sledge, the volunteers were positioned at ten-yard intervals along the length of the track. In theory, this meant that each puller had the same weight added to the sledge at the same point. When the tractor ground to a halt, the 'pull' was considered over. The distance travelled was measured and the step-on volunteers were then required to resume their trackside positions, ready for the next puller's attempt.

However, in practice, if a volunteer wanted to go home or had simply had enough, replacement volunteers were never an accurate substitute for the weight which had 'gone home'. Competition then became unfair, and many pullers would go home in tears. Nevertheless, tractor pulling with a step-on sledge proved to be faster and more entertaining than the slow, dead-weight pulling method.

Tractors used in these pulls were similar in sophistication to the sledge, and pulling was considered a 'pull on Sunday, plough on Monday' affair, using the same tractor.

The biggest tractor pulling event during the 1960s was at the M & W Power Show, which was billed, somewhat inaccurately, as there were only American competitors, as the World Championships. Until this time, tractor pulling was strictly a standard farm tractor event, but as everyone wanted to win, the tractors were soon subjected to tune-ups. Commonly, turbochargers were added and fuel injection pumps were uprated and these 'tuned-up' stock tractors became the forerunners of today's super stock competition tractors. Other pullers changed engines, squeezing high-powered V8 engines into the chassis of a standard tractor, and these eventually became known as modified tractors.

Paul Bosse with his modified tractor in action at the Ohio State Fair in 1974 — a McCormick Farmall fitted with a 460 cubic inch Ford V8 engine.

By this time, the principle of the step-on sledge was well and truly accepted, but as tractor power increased through these modifications, a speed limit had to be imposed to maintain some element of safety for volunteers when stepping on to the moving sledge. Using a pace tractor, each pull was then restricted to a maximum speed of six miles per hour.

As there was so much controversy over the accuracy of the step-on sledge because of its constantly changing volunteers as ballast, sledge builders needed a more accurate method of applying a progressive load to each pulling tractor as it moved along the track. Whatever the method, it was imperative that the load remain identical for each competitor, so there would be no squabbling over changes in sledge ballast. This saw the introduction of mechanical weight transfer sledges—which still required the use of a pace tractor—and Billy Watkins' special mechanical set-up was the first weight transfer sledge design to be patented.

The year 1969 proved to be a big turning point in American tractor pulling. The sport had progressed considerably from its simple beginnings and was in need of a governing body to maintain direction and stipulate a few rules. So, eight American states (Illinois, Indiana, Iowa, Michigan, Minnesota, Missouri, Ohio and Pennsylvania) joined forces to form the National Tractor Pullers Association (NTPA). On 12 and 13 April 1969, the first formal meeting of the NTPA, with Ed Hart as the first president, was held at the Ramada Inn in Ottawa, Illinois, to establish the first set of uniform rules for the sport of tractor pulling.

At this time the NTPA introduced two pulling divisions, stock and modified. It was not until five years later, in 1974, that an additional division—the modified mini tractors—was introduced. The nature of the sport required that the tractor's weight play as

Noble Harrison pioneered the use of two-stage turbocharging with his Allis-Chalmers tractor. Note the use of a smoke extraction system above the tractor.

Solid Junk driven by Dave Stangle, an early alcohol-based tractor.

(*Below*)
In 1973 John Thompson was Hypermax's first customer and his International 1466 featured a water-injection system designed by Jerry Lagod, which was to benefit the tractor's two-stage turbocharging.

Danny Dean's Rooster was also a Hypermax-powered tractor.

important a part as the production of horsepower, so it came to be that within these stock and modified tractor divisions, there would be specific maximum weight classes for tractors of 5000 lb, 7000 lb, 9000 lb, 12,000 lb and 15,000 lb including fuel, ballast and driver weight.

Tractor tuning also took considerable leaps during these early years, for it was in 1969 that the first two-stage turbocharged tractor, an Allis-Chalmers 220 owned by Noble Harrison of Illinois, appeared on the scene. However, this breakthrough in the use of turbochargers took time and effort to refine, as this new level of engine tuning had never been tried before, and it was another eight years before other pullers ventured beyond the level of two-stage turbocharging.

Despite the NTPA being formed only one year earlier, 1970 was the first year that end-of-season points champions were declared. With tractor pulling gaining such a strong following, the NTPA looked to find a way of keeping pullers and spectators informed of developments, so an association newsletter or magazine was to be produced.

Called *The Puller*, this sprang from a project by Kay Hart Wagner while attending Ohio State University. The first issue consisted of 11 pages and was considered more of a newsletter than a magazine. However, as the sport continued to grow, so did the newsletter, eventually totalling 64 pages and reaching an audience on two continents. It was 'the voice' of tractor pulling.

During the early 1970s, tractors competing in the stock division began to reveal very interesting developments. For the first time, pullers were experimenting with alcohol as an alternative fuel to diesel: it burned colder, so engine components were less likely to melt, but, more importantly, it resulted in greater power outputs.

Stock tractors using a combination of liquid petroleum gas and alcohol were pioneered by Illinois pullers Don Nolan, Harold Jennings and Earl Small, who were quickly followed by Ron Perry of Indiana, and JR Herriot of Illinois, who built an alcohol-burning tractor called Solid Junk which was driven by Dave Stangle. However, to this present day, alcohol remains a minority fuel for stock pulling tractors, with diesel being the preferred fuel. Interestingly, alcohol-burning stock tractors have yet to make an impact on British tractor pulling, having been tried out with little

The crossbox. Following on from Carl and Paul Bosse's early design introduced in 1973, the modern-day crossbox has allowed pullers to keep on adding engines to tractors.

success by Paul and Alan Williams with their pro stock tractor Leyland Lady and Andrew Gilbert with his Massey Ferguson tractor built to run on cane fuel.

Modified tractors moved forward in 1971 with the introduction of the 1710 cubic inch (28 litre) V12 Allison engine, sourced from 1940s aircraft. The first Allison-powered tractor had just the one engine and was built by Illinois pullers Bob Bend and Fred Mende. That same year saw the 'Bend and Mende' team win a points title with their unique aircraft-engined tractor.

Tractor pulling was full of controversy during these early years. In the middle of the 1971 season, two clutch and flywheel assemblies exploded and at the resulting NTPA executive board meeting, the decision was made to ban all automotive V8-engined modified tractors from competition until they were equipped with bellhousings, flywheels, clutches and automatic transmissions approved by SEMA (Speciality Equipment Market Association).

Fireworks followed as this 'new rule' was policed at a tractor pull at Monroe, Michigan, where not one modified tractor was equipped with the approved components, and pullers were informed that tractors would not be allowed to run until they had

Art Arfons on board his single turbine-engined tractor with only ear defenders for company. Art started tractor pulling with turbine engines in 1974.

Norm Green revolutionised super stock pulling in 1977 with his Allis-Chalmers D 21. It featured four turbochargers and was a serious threat to the dominance of the Hypermax-powered International Harvester tractors.

fitted the necessary approved parts.

It is reported that the following evening, the pullers held a meeting to try to strike a deal with the fair organisers. Illinois rules director Martin Graf and NTPA president Ed Hart were present, and, on their advice, the fair board told pullers there would be no sanction or insurance unless the approved components were fitted.

This resulted in only a few tractors running that evening, and with tempers running high, Martin Graf and Ed Hart were escorted out of the fair ground—and out of the state—by police, until the situation had diffused. This incident was regarded as one of the most critical in the NTPA's history and it established the authority of officers to make rulings on any safety matters that might arise.

Jerry Lagod, a highly skilled engineer, opened his business called Hypermax in 1972. This was to have a tremendous impact on the stock tractor division, giving big power dividends for pullers using International Harvester tractors. It was the start of battles between the 'red' tractors and all other makes of stock tractor. Hypermax was (and still is) to tractor pulling what Red Rum was to horse racing.

By 1973, Jerry Lagod's first tractor pulling customer, John Thompson, appeared on the scene with the first stock tractor with Hypermax engineering under the bonnet, and this proved to

be a massive breakthrough in diesel engine tuning. Thompson's tractor, a two-stage turbocharged IH 1466, featured the first water-injection system matched to a high-performance diesel engine, and this was Jerry Lagod's first serious contribution to tractor pulling.

Reports in *The Puller* magazine explained how this new water-injection system on Thompson's diesel engine was used to lower the high air temperature generated by the two-stage turbocharger system without causing an inlet restriction on the engine. Without the water injection, the boost pressure and high temperatures generated in multi-turbocharged diesel engines would melt or destroy everything downstream of the turbochargers.

However, Lagod's innovative breakthrough in diesel engine tuning was not visible for all to see, as it was concealed by side panels fitted to Thompson's tractor. This earned his tractor the nickname of Silver Shields and started a trend which has led to many pullers displaying murals on the sides of their tractors.

In the same year, pullers Danny Dean of Ohio and Dickie Sullivan of Missouri, impressed by Lagod's work, followed Thompson along the road to Hypermax. This route to high horsepower was quickly taken up by other pullers using International Harvester tractors, and tractor pulling in the stock division, particularly after the advent of Hypermax technology, started to see the man with the deepest pockets getting the most wins.

As Jerry Lagod's involvement in tractor pulling grew quickly

Neil Wagner at Fort Recovery, Ohio, in 1979 with his twin Allison-engined tractor. This engine configuration is now recognised as stair-stepped.

through the 1970s and into the 1980s—Hypermax is still big business in the States—IH factory-research money poured into his business. This resulted in 'red' tractors winning the majority of pulls, particularly in the heavier classes.

As more pullers adopted the two-stage turbocharger set-up, the word 'super' was added to the stock tractor division's name and the super stock tractor was born. This is no ploughing tractor; it is a thoroughbred machine developed strictly for competition use.

While super stock tractors were keeping their panels, for engine secrecy and decorative reasons, modified tractors were losing theirs. Bonnets, side panels and grilles were considered an inconvenient and immovable weight which could not be easily repositioned to gain the best weight distribution on the tractor. There seemed little point in having decorative panels on the front of the tractor when weight was needed over the back axle for extra traction.

In 1973, Carl and Paul Bosse of Ohio introduced the crossbox for tractors in the modified division, which was a development of what Carl Bosse had seen in military applications where two Cadillac engines were used in a tank. The crossbox allowed pullers to link up any number of engines to a single drive train and this development turned out to be one of the single most valuable introductions for tractor pulling, paving the way for today's multi-engined tractors now running in the modified division. The Bosse Brothers used the crossbox in their tractor to link up four 460 cubic inch (7.5 litre) Ford engines—a tractor which won the 1973 Grand National points title.

The Banter Brothers of Indiana, using a modified tractor, took

Les Grodi in action during 1981 with only six engines. In 1982, he returned to the circuit with an eight-engined tractor.

the first of their many points titles and by the close of the 1992 pulling season had added a further 18 titles to the first and were recognised as the most consistent winners in the sport.

The first Indianapolis (Indy) super pull took place in 1974, and eight competitors—four in super stock and four in modified—took home top prizes. This has since turned into an annual event held every January, and it is to tractor pulling what the superbowl is to American football. In order to compete at this event, pullers must first qualify.

The year 1974 also saw the introduction of the modified mini tractors, which were subsequently recognised as the NTPA's third tractor pulling division and were allocated 1500 lb and 1700 lb weight classes. At this same time, tractor pulling acquired a legendary motor-sport name for its fast-growing list of competitors—Art Arfons. Together with Bob Frock of Ohio, Arfons debuted the first single turbine-engined tractor, competing in the modified division.

This, coinciding with the elimination of the pace tractor, turned tractor pulling into a very high horsepower sport. The most notable change in pulling 'technique' was a dramatic increase in wheel speeds—this change allowed competitors to get the sledge moving quickly off the line and use its weight and higher forward speed as momentum to help the pulling tractor when the weight transfer load increased. By 1975, modern day tractor pulling was well and truly underway.

The following season, the Banter Brothers competed with the first modified tractor that used two supercharged 427 cubic inch (7.0 litre) Chevrolet engines. As pulling progressed, so did the Banter Brothers. In time, they had the first triple-engined tractor, and by 1980 they had moved on to four engines and later to five and then six engines, all equipped with superchargers. Currently, the Banter Brothers pulling team competes with two modified tractors; Mr. Chevy and The Bandit. Both tractors are equipped with six supercharged 454 cubic inch (7.5 litre) Chevrolet engines and they compete in the NTPA's unlimited class.

However, the introduction of multi-engined modified tractors and highly tuned super stock tractors was taking its toll on transmission components and clutches. Enter the 'slipper' or 'automatic' clutch, which allowed pullers to engage a gear without having to depress the clutch pedal.

Like a conventional clutch, the slipper clutch uses plates, but that is where the similarity stops. Unlike a conventional clutch which relies on spring pressure from a cover plate to hold the drive, the slipper clutch relies on centrifugal force to 'throw' weights out towards the circumference of the clutch. This throwing action compresses the clutch plates together. So, the higher the rpm, the tighter the clutch locks up, eliminating any possibility of clutch slip at high rpm.

Slipper clutch actuation, then, can be conventionally, by releasing the clutch pedal while bringing up engine revs, or by

Hyper Tension, Norm Green's Allis-Chalmers D 21, in action at Toma in 1984.

simply opening the throttle to get the clutch to lock up.

An additional pulling division appeared during 1976. The four-wheel drive division and vehicles pulled initially in two weight classes, with a restriction on maximum engine capacity of 650 cubic inches (10.6 litres). Superchargers were not allowed. This division has since been streamlined from 5000 lb and 6000 lb weight classes to a single 6200 lb weight class, and represents the NTPA's fourth pulling division. In the interests of safety, kill switches, which had been haphazardly in use since the start of the 1970s, were written into the rule book and made a mandatory requirement in all pulling classes.

The following season was a significant one in the development of the sport of tractor pulling. Mild steel tubular chassis designs appeared among modified tractors and resulted in lightweight chassis with incredible strength. The weight saving allowed the use of additional engines, while previously heavy, yet powerful, tractors could shed sufficient weight to compete in the lighter weight classes. In the same year, the NTPA adopted the term Grand National Circuit and the end-of-season point champions were referred to as Grand National champions. Mike Miller of Illinois, seeing what Art Arfons had previously achieved with a single turbine-engined tractor, took turbine engine technology a step further in tractor pulling with his new twin turbine-engined tractor.

With the body raised, the engine and driving position can be clearly seen in this two-wheel drive truck.

Indoor pulling with the super stock division.

As indoor pulling is more confined than outdoor events, safety must be stepped up. Here, it can be seen that two sledge chains are in use for extra safety — should the primary chain break, the pulling vehicle will be retained by the secondary chain. This is a top priority where the end of the track finishes abruptly with a sand bank and the stadium wall.

Four-wheel drive pulling in action.

Later that same season, Norm Green, with the help of Bob Mitchell and Al Kock, increased the horsepower of super stock tractors. Green's tractor, an Allis-Chalmers D-21, was the first to feature four turbochargers under the bonnet and represented a serious threat to the dominance of the Hypermax-powered International Harvesters, 'spannered' by Jerry Lagod. Under present super stock rules, this is the maximum number of turbochargers allowed and the turbochargers must be 'arranged' to create a maximum of three pressure stages.

Also in 1977, for the first time since the evolution of motorised tractor pulling in the 1920s, the sport ventured out of America and into Europe.

A demonstration tractor pull, held at the World Ploughing Championship at Flevohof, Holland, was supported by Lester Houck and Mark Stauffer from Pennsylvania, who transported their tractors Foxy Lady and Sneeki Pete across to Europe to take part in the Flevohof pull. From here, Foxy Lady changed hands and never returned to America.

This demonstration pull was attended, coincidentally, by Tom and Mark Osborne from Romsey, Hampshire, and Mike Hansard from Lincolnshire. All three were to have their influence on tractor pulling's public introduction in Britain during the follow ing year.

Back in the States, the following season saw a first for female pullers. Julie Sporhase from Colorado had broken into what had previously been a male-dominated sport and quickly cemented her determination by qualifying for the following January's Indy Super Pull.

With no pace tractor to restrict pulling speed, the once-powerful single V12 Allison aircraft engines being used in modified tractors were quickly becoming outclassed by the supercharged multi-engined tractors. With this in mind, Mike Holden of Ohio uprated his single Allison-engined tractor with the first twin turbocharger set-up for Allison engines, while Neil Wagner, also from Ohio, skipped the use of turbochargers and opted to build a twin Allison-engined modified tractor.

By the 1980s, tractor pulling had accelerated in popularity and this was enhanced by the NTPA's official recognition of pro stock tractors in 1981. The pro stock division became the NTPA's fifth pulling division with weight classes of 10,000 lb and 12,000 lb. Despite being outwardly similar to the super stock tractors, the pro stocks were—and still are—limited to a maximum of one turbocharger.

For 1982, modified tractor pulling saw the development of an eight-engined tractor owned by Les Grodi of Michigan. At the time, *The Puller* magazine was noted for its comment, 'It must be a mechanic's nightmare to tune.' The next season saw two-wheel drive vehicles competing at the track and this was the sixth and last division to join the NTPA. The two-wheel drive division, like the four-wheel drive division, was given weight classes of 5000 lb

erry Dabbs from Stuttgart, Arkansas, in the mini division. The weight limit for NTPA mini tractors is 1800 lb.

and 6000 lb. It, too, has now been streamlined to one 6200 lb class and also has a 650 cubic inch (10.6 litre) maximum engine capacity, with the use of only one supercharger. During 1983 the pro stock, four-wheel drive and mini modified divisions were invited to take part in the Indy Super Pull.

By 1984, the North American Sledge Operators Association (NASOA) was officially incorporated into the NTPA, and took on the responsibility of inspecting and licensing sledges for competition use at NTPA sanctioned events, and in the following year, at an NTPA board meeting in Chicago, World Pulling International Inc (WPI) was formed as a stockholder's company to handle the business affairs of the NTPA.

Eight years after Mike Holden introduced twin turbochargers on Allison engines, he again moved forward in the modified tractor pulling division in 1986 with the first tractor to feature three V12 Allison engines. (Two years later he built a tractor equipped with four Allison engines.) Also in 1986, Tim Engler from Indiana, rampaged through the modified division with a Grand National points title in each of the four modified weight classes; it is an achievement yet to be equalled by any other tractor puller.

Two years later, Tim Engler was the first puller to operate a seven-engined tractor fitted with superchargers, and major sponsorship from US Tobacco saw the rise of the Copenhagen/SKOAL Pulling Circuit.

In 1989, Gardner Stone, a tractor puller with years of experience competing with Allison-powered tractors, debuted the first modified tractor using four turbine engines called General Stage IV. This tractor earned Stone a Grand National title one year

Judy Knipstein from Fort Wayne, Indiana, is one of a growing number of lady drivers in the NTPA's modified division.

The Arias-powered Irish Challenger is one of three pulling vehicles run by the Walsh family.

Bryan and Ernie Conner from Missouri compete with Bad Medicine, an alcohol-burning super stock tractor. Its engine started life as a standard V8 Caterpillar 3208 diesel engine, but now runs on alcohol and has three turbochargers. It can be seen that alky burners don't smoke like 'traditional' diesel-fuelled super stocks.

Russ Mears from Cynthiana, Ohio, driving his super stock tractor Just Maybe, a Case International 7130. Smoke extraction is essential when super stocks pull indoors.

later. The SFI (a development from SEMA) joined forces with the NTPA to assist in maintaining tractor pulling's record of safety. SFI is responsible for developing and administrating minimum performance standards for automotive components for personal and vehicle safety. Examples of components with SFI specifications include helmets, firesuits, flywheels and shatter blankets.

The dominance of Hypermax-powered 'red' tractors in the super stock division is, to a large extent, still maintained despite many other super stock tractors going down the 'four turbo' route in the search for maximum power. By 1989, the International Harvester dominated with 35 Grand National points titles, compared with 16 titles for Allis-Chalmers, three for Minneapolis Moline and two for John Deere.

In her first appearance at an Indy Super Pull in 1991, Rodalyn Knox became the first woman to win an Indy title, pulling in the unlimited weight class of the modified division. She also finished third in the Grand National points race for 1991 and second during 1992, and begs the question—could 1993 be Rodalyn Knox's year?

In 1992, the NTPA had in excess of 800 pulling vehicles registered, with almost 1200 competing members, taking part in the NTPA's four pulling circuits. And there were 21 member states within the NTPA.

For 1993, the NTPA is sanctioning six divisions of pulling tractor in eleven weight classes. These are as follows:

- modified in 5800 lb, 7200 lb and an unlimited class
- super stock in 5500 lb, 7500 lb and 9500 lb weight classes
- pro stock in 10,000 lb and 12,000 lb weight classes
- two-wheel drive in the 6200 lb weight class
- four-wheel drive in the 6200 lb weight class
- mini modified in the 1800 lb weight class

Over and above the pulling divisions and weight classes, the NTPA sanctions tractor pulling at four levels of competition. The NTPA's showcase event is the Grand National Copenhagen/SKOAL Pulling Circuit, which in 1992 was a 13 event circuit offering prize money totalling some $160,200 paid out to the top ten places in two-wheel drive, four-wheel drive, super stock and unlimited divisions, and to the top five places in the modified mini division.

The additional three levels of competition are Pro National, State National and State, and statistics show a total attendance figure for the 1991 season, for all levels of competition, of 1,619,448. During 1992, the 13 event Grand National circuit alone attracted a total of 243,750 spectators.

The British Tractor Pullers Association

Tractor pulling made its first public appearance in the United Kingdom in 1978, with a demonstration pull at the Royal Show, at Stoneleigh, Warwickshire, although its real introduction occurred over 12 months earlier.

During 1977, Mark Osborne, son of Hampshire agricultural machinery dealer Tom Osborne of A.T. Osborne, stumbled across an article on American tractor pulling in a car magazine. His enthusiasm and curiosity about this new and fascinating motor sport with farm tractors led him to convince his father that tractor pulling could be started in the UK.

Having sold his father some ideas, Mark, together with Steve Kelly, an apprentice with A.T. Osborne, set about building a pulling tractor from various parts of machinery in their yard. Shire Lady, as the tractor was eventually named, was quite literally cobbled together using a Muir Hill rear axle and torque converter transmission; a Ford 360 cubic inch (5.8 litre), six-cylinder diesel engine, which was fully rebuilt for its new purpose; and a Ransomes combine harvester, which kindly donated one of its axles to give the tractor a pair of front wheels.

With his tractor in 'running order', Mark took to the fields to experiment, thinking about what he could pull to really test its ability.

A sledge was needed, but with only a few photocopied pictures from a car magazine for reference, it looked as though this could be a long, uphill struggle.

The Osborne's business activities in the agricultural industry meant that a forthcoming event such as the World Ploughing Championship at Flevohof, Holland, would not pass unnoticed. An advertisement for the event carried information on a tractor pulling demonstration which was to be held alongside the ploughing match and was to feature tractors and a sledge from the American tractor pulling circuit. So it was decided that Tom, Mark and Steve Kelly, armed with sketch pads and cameras, would go to Holland.

At the World Ploughing Championship, the tractor pulling demonstration proved, at best, disappointing, as it was held on concrete which is the most unsuitable surface for tractors trying to get grip. However, this gave Tom the opportunity to talk to the

Tractor No. 1 pulling sledge No. 1 in 1978, both owned by Tom and Mark Osborne. Mark is driving Shire Lady.

Tom Osborne.

Foxy Lady, owned by Dutchman Maurits Immink, was among the few taking part in the first 'public' tractor pull at the Royal Show, Stoneleigh, in 1978.

(*Above*)
Jay Forrester competed in many British tractor pulls. On this occasion, he was driving his modified tractor Boss Mustang powered by two Ford V8 engines. Primrose Rovers is among the tractors in the background.

An early tractor pull in Lancashire with Stan Cookson's sledge and the Funky Gibbon. Track boundaries and spectator areas were yet to be defined.

people involved—there was already a growing interest in the sport in Holland—and to take many close-up photographs of how the sledge was built. More importantly, the group learnt how the weight transfer sledge worked and came away feeling more than confident that tractor pulling would soon be a recognised motor sport in Britain.

Back at their workshop, Tom and the lads set about building a sledge for use with the tractor. After many hours spent burning the midnight oil, the first British-built sledge appeared. Like the sledge seen in Holland, this was based on an HGV trailer and comprised a skid pan at the front, a ballast box which could move, on rails, up and down the length of the trailer and a small auxiliary engine which could be used to reset the ballast box at the rear of the sledge (over the trailer's wheels) after a pull had been made.

Out in the field, Mark hitched his tractor to the sledge and then pulled. Fortunately, everything on the sledge worked exactly as it had been designed to do. So Mark pulled again, then again and again. The result was a positive breakthrough in the development of British tractor pulling.

The next step forward was to establish some basic rules on what could and could not be done while taking part in the sport. Tom got hold of a copy of the 1977 NTPA rule book and several issues of *The Puller* from the United States, which further helped an understanding of how tractor pulling should take place.

Not long after this, the BBC television programme 'Tomorrow's World' found out about the Osbornes' involvement in tractor pulling and went to Hampshire to investigate. With BBC personnel as the audience, the Osbornes put on a demonstration using their newly built tractor and sledge combination. As a result, they were invited to London—with tractor and sledge—to perform a live demonstration for broadcast by 'Tomorrow's World' on this new motor sport called tractor pulling.

In the weeks following the programme, Tom Osborne received countless telephone calls from people who had seen the programme and were interested to find out more about this new pastime. One call was from the Royal Agricultural Society of England (RASE) expressing an interest in demonstrating the sport at the forthcoming Royal Show. As a result of that telephone call, Tom Osborne arranged to meet representatives of the RASE and Jimmy Harrison from Goodyear Great Britain at the 1977 Smithfield Show in London and, following this meeting, it was agreed that the Royal Show held at Stoneleigh, Warwickshire, would play host to a demonstration tractor pull in July 1978. It was now up to Tom Osborne: this was his big break, a shop window for the sport, but he had less than seven months to work on his sledge and to find the number of tractors which would make the demonstration work over the Royal Show's four-day duration.

Meanwhile, Lincolnshire tractor dealer Mike Hansard of the

Holton Tractor Co Ltd exported tractors to the United States. His American business contact, Jay Forrester of Chambersburg, Pennsylvania, was already tractor pulling and introduced Mike to the sport while on one of his many business trips to the US in 1975. Mike frequently joined Jay at tractor pulls, but his personal involvement with the sport did not go any further until after the World Ploughing Championship at Flevohof, Holland in 1977.

After Mike saw tractor pulling in Holland, he knew it was destined for the UK. And on more than one occasion, Jay tried to persuade Mike that he was the man to launch tractor pulling before a British audience, but Mike, because of work commitments, felt he was too busy to put in sufficient time to promote such a new and unknown sport to a traditionally reserved British public. Mike had enjoyed the tractor pulling he had seen with Jay in the US—having driven Jay's tractor on more than one occasion—and was happy to dwell on his overseas experiences.

However, not long after the World Ploughing event, Mike heard about Tom Osborne's planned demonstration of tractor pulling at the 1978 Royal Show. Thinking back to his business trips to the US and the tractor pulling with Jay, he knew what was about to unfold, so he decided to support Tom, and so set about preparing his own tractor for the event. Mike's first pulling tractor was a Ford 7000—a four-cylinder turbocharged, factory-produced tractor complete with cab. With the help of Jay, Mike was able to apply some American tractor pulling technology to his tractor: a bigger turbocharger, wider tyres and an uprated diesel injector pump. This would make the tractor rev to over twice its factory-set 2500 rpm limit and with an uprated fuel system would give Mike some real horsepower.

Mike's tractor, known as Lincoln Way—named as a gesture to Jay Forrester, whose business traded from Lincoln Way—was prepared for the big demonstration.

At the 1978 Royal Show, Jimmy Harrison and Gordon Davies, supported 100 per cent by their employer, Goodyear Great Britain, and helped by Arthur Phelps, a good friend of Tom Osborne, who later was to be known as Mr Rule Book, supplied flags and marked out a track on a piece of ground allocated by the show organisers. Goodyear also fitted new tyres to those tractors taking part in the event. This was the very first British tractor pull and comprised five tractors on the first day of the show: Shire Lady driven by Mark Osborne, Lincoln Way driven by Mike Hansard, The Funky Gibbon driven by Tony Bourne, Eltrac Deutz owned by George Lyons and Foxy Lady owned by Dutchman Maurits Immink. Foxy Lady was an American tractor purchased by Maurits after its appearance at the World Ploughing Championship at Flevohof in the previous autumn.

People came from all over the show ground to investigate the noise and smoke being created and the event proved to be a

Woodhall Warrior, an early diesel-powered modified tractor.

Before the introduction of a 'track side weighbridge', pullers were trusted to weigh-in at public weighbridges en-route to a pull, producing a ticket as proof of tractor weight. The tractor is the legendary Packard-engined Snoopy, built and owned by Mick Cushing.

The interest generated at the Royal Show prompted many farmers to try pulling with their standard tractors. For some, once was enough, but many returned to later pulls with more ambitious tractors.

(*Below*)
Mike Hansard driving Lincoln Way I at the Town and Country Festival in 1978. Jay Forrester provided the smoke.

definite crowd puller. On the Tuesday, Wednesday and Thursday of the Royal Show, farmers returned with their own tractors, eager to have a go at pulling the sledge, and this involvement was eventually to see the introduction of a Farmer's division.

The RASE expressed disappointment over the lack of true 'pulling tractors' that had taken part, despite continued operation of sledge and tractors without breaking down. Tom Osborne, however, was very pleased with the way the demonstration had progressed. The tractors and sledge performed well and, equally important, throughout the four days there was a large crowd by the track and interest in tractor pulling was boosted by a surprising number of people who wanted to build their own tractors and join in. Tom thus went back to Hampshire and decided to form a club on the strength of the enquiries from the Royal Show demonstration.

On a similar theme to the United States' National Tractor Pullers Association (NTPA), Tom Osborne set up the British Tractor Pullers Association (BTPA). Its logo sprang from that of the NTPA, but using the Union Jack and the word 'British' instead of 'National'. It was a simple design that any country could easily adopt using its name and flag. Tom reasoned that with a generic identity, tractor pulling could soon have worldwide recognition.

A British rule book based on that of the NTPA soon followed and was posted out to all those who enquired after the Royal Show demonstration.

The August Bank Holiday after the Royal Show saw agricultural contractor Stan Cookson put on a tractor pull at Great Eccleston in the north-west of England. The Royal Show had been an ideal opportunity for Stan to meet Tom Osborne and explain how he was producing a sledge to operate in his region. Seeing Tom's sledge in action, Stan was able to put the finishing touches to his own sledge, and with support from many friends and colleagues, Stan was able to get tractor pulling up and running in Lancashire. He was supported by pullers from the Royal Show event and had numerous other tractors taking part which, it seemed, had joined in straight from the farm yard.

Later that year, Tom Osborne and John Bowen-Jones, an agricultural machinery dealer from Northamptonshire, went to Holland and met up with Dutch tractor puller Jan Buitenhuis and his allies. John was a spectator at the first event and, as a good friend of Tom's, quickly became involved in other aspects of the sport.

The Dutch were looking to form a tractor pulling organisation in Holland and the BTPA rule book was an ideal focal point for all to follow. Both Tom and John wanted the same rules to be applicable to all tractor pullers, reasoning that tractors could then compete in other countries when a common rule book was in force.

In the years that followed, these rules, in a more up-to-date form, became known as the European Tractor Pulling Committee (ETPC) rule book, and, as initially perceived by Tom Osborne, British tractors started to appear at events throughout Europe.

In the winter months after that first Royal Show pull, Mike Hansard, John Bowen-Jones and Tom Osborne went to America to visit Jay Forrester. As Jay's guests, they attended several pulls in Pennsylvania and a lot was learnt about additional NTPA rules and regulations, which were then implemented in the UK. The same visit gave John the information he needed to build a sledge, following on from the development of his first tractor Helmdon Rocket.

The next tractor pull at the Royal Show took place in the following year and had more tractors, more direction and a lot more interest. The RASE had decided to move the track further away from its first roadside location to give spectators more room and it seemed that the winter months spent studying and updating the rule book had paid off handsomely.

Tractor numbers had increased considerably from the first five 'pulling tractors' of the previous year. The Osbornes were now running two additional tractors—a second super stock known as Moonshine and a modified tractor called Forest Bootlegger. A guest appearance by Jay Forrester with his super stock tractor helped to stir up crowd enthusiasm.

One of the many new pulling tractors at this second event was Mike Cushing's Snoopy, a modified tractor powered by a Packard engine—a tractor which was several years ahead of its time (now called Short Circuit and owned by Julian Leese, this tractor still competes in a rebuilt and revised form using the same engine). The Funkies returned with their Massey Ferguson 590 the Funky Gibbon, now with two turbochargers, and the Creed Brothers appeared with their first version of Hardwick Beast, powered at that time by two diesel engines.

There was no on-site method of weighing tractors at a pull, so those taking part were trusted to use a public weighbridge en-route to a pull and produce a ticket as confirmation of tractor weight in order to participate in the weight classes of 5000 lb, 7000 lb, 9000 lb and 12,000 lb.

Following the success of this second pull at the Royal Show, it was decided that tractor pulling needed a regular circuit around the country. This would give tractor pullers more opportunities to take part in more than one pull each year and, equally as important, would put the sport in front of a greater audience.

As the sport was relatively unknown, it seemed sensible to introduce it to the public at established shows, so county events such as steam fairs, rallies and local agricultural shows were targeted by the BTPA. But according to Tom Osborne, this was not easy, as show organisers and officials were difficult to captivate and were often too concerned with the noise created at pulls rather than the large number of spectators it easily gathered. On the few occasions that tractor pulling appeared at

(*Above*)
Bounty Hunter is one of two pulling trucks registered with the BTPA. Owned by the Stone Brothers, this D-Series Ford has twin V8 Chevrolet power behind the cab.

The second is Noddy Truck, currently owned by Tony Bruegger. Power is from a six-cylinder, two-stage turbocharged Scania engine. A mixture of methanol and diesel helps to provide the power.

(*Above*)
Peter Clarke's successful Windbush was rebuilt and re-panelled to become Bull Power, a super stock tractor with three-stage turbocharging. Decision Maker, the sledge, is Tom Osborne's original under Mike Lawrence's ownership.

Gandalf was Jim Snell's first pulling tractor and used only four straight-six Jaguar engines.

other events, the site proved inadequate in track, pit area and spectator room, and as public safety was a top priority, pulls became increasingly harder to effect.

The Bath and West Show Ground in Somerset refused to have anything to do with tractor pulling, as did Ashton Court near Bristol, although this latter venue became involved during the following year and has been strongly supportive ever since. The Festival of Transport Show at Yeovil, Somerset, also welcomed tractor pulling and is still in favour of its appearance on an annual basis—in 1992, the sandy-based track at Yeovil was refurbished with clay to reduce the abrasiveness and add excitement to the venue.

Around the country, there were—and still are—many possible sites for tractor pulling, whether in supporting shows or standing alone. However, many show committees were reluctant to give up the large area of land required to install a track with adequate room for spectators and a pit area, and many proved to be lethargic in coming up with prize monies and travelling expenses for pullers.

After all, it was the competitors that put on the show and they were the ones who had to bear the cost of transporting their tractors around the country. They were the ones who increased attendance figures at many events, and without the continued assistance and support from their one major sponsor, Goodyear Great Britain, the BTPA could well have failed to get properly established.

It seemed that outside the 'hard core' of followers, there was little public and media interest in what is now recognised as the world's most powerful motor sport. However, persistence and a desire to see more tractor pulls take place began to pay off for the BTPA.

By 1980, four sledges were registered for competition use and were ideally located around the country so that one sledge did not have to be transported to the various pulling venues in the UK. Sledge No.1 belonged to Tom Osborne in Hampshire and covered southern events. Sledge No.2 belonged to Stan Cookson of Lancashire and was used at northern tractor pulls. Sledge No.3 was Fred Henley's of Yorkshire and was used at events in the Midlands, as was sledge No.4 which belonged to John Bowen-Jones of Northants.

Throughout 1980, the BTPA was chaired by Tom Osborne with Mike Cushing as vice-chairman, Tony Bourne as treasurer, John Bowen-Jones as events organiser, Arthur Phelps as head track marshall, Gordon Davies as head scrutineer and Paul Flackett for publicity. Remaining committee members at that time were Mike Hansard, George Lyons, Ken Smith, Terry Barnsley and Harold Hewitt.

After several newsletters in 1979 and 1980, *The British Puller* magazine was launched. Serving primarily as a newsletter to members, the magazine was quickly made available to spectators, being sold track-side at pulls. Its frequency was varied at that time, but has now settled as an annual publication with around 3000 copies sold throughout the pulling season.

The BTPA's 1980 fixture list had grown to 14 venues with two additional proposed venues, of which eight had tractor pulling scheduled as two, three and four day events. And of the total number of scheduled events, seven were British championship points pulls. The first event of the season was set for Saturday, 12 April at Ardingly, West Sussex, and the season was to conclude with a proposed pull at Helmdon, Northants, on Sunday, 28 September.

The following year, the events list had increased to 19 venues, again with seven events scheduled as points pulls for the British championship title.

With the continued introduction of new pulling vehicles from a never-ending stream of people wanting to become tractor pullers, the BTPA found itself with almost 50 competing vehicles. This was becoming increasingly difficult to manage as a voluntary club, and as people needed to look after their own business first, the BTPA was often viewed as a secondary requirement. At this stage, its affairs really needed to be looked after on a professional basis, as the amount of time and devotion the sport needed could no longer be supplied by pullers on an evening/weekend basis.

But, there was no way the BTPA could afford to take on employees to organise and run tractor pulling. The answer then was to split membership into regional clubs up and down the country. Each club would have its own chairman and committee members, who would be answerable to a governing body at the BTPA. In time, these clubs became recognised as the North West, Midlands, East Midlands and South West tractor pullers clubs, to be joined by the mini tractor pullers club in 1987. Currently, four clubs remain, as the East Midlands and Midlands clubs now tend to operate as one, and there are four regularly used tracks in the BTPA's tractor pulling circuit.

Tom Osborne's activities with the BTPA concluded in the mid 1980s. His business demanded too much of his own time and there was also the expense of running three tractors and a sledge. He wanted to let a younger man with high enthusiasm and, more importantly, plenty of spare time take over. His tractors were dismantled and the sledge was sold on to tractor puller and haulage contractor Mike Lawrence in Somerset.

Since then the Osborne family has not returned to competitive tractor pulling, but is happy to maintain contact and occasionally attend events around the country. There are many other pullers too who have come and gone over the years, retiring for financial, business or other reasons and tractors have either been broken up, sold or simply parked in a dark corner of a shed.

For the 1993 tractor pulling season, the BTPA has over 50 registered pulling vehicles, and pulling divisions are minis, pro stock, super stock and modified. There is also pulling with two-wheel drive trucks—a slow-growing class in which there are currently only two vehicles, Noddy Truck and Bounty Hunter. Weight classes are currently 900 kg for mini modified tractors, 3400 kg and 4400 kg for both pro stock and super stock tractors, while the modified division competes in 2400 kg, 3400 kg, 4400 kg and 5400 kg (reduced from 5700 kg on 1 January 1993 at the request of the ETPC).

Among pullers, weight classes are still referred to as the '5', '7', '9' and '12' as a result of the early imperial weight classification, although those more familiar with the metric classes abbreviate the current weight classes to 'two-four', 'three-four', 'four-four' and 'five-seven' (now of course 'five-four').

The BTPA's early logo design. It is still in use for stickers.

Designed for the '90s, the BTPA's new logo.

BRITISH TRACTOR PULLERS ASSOCIATION

Sledges and Tracks

Sledges

It has to be said that without a sledge, there would be no tractor pulling. The roar and smoke made by multi-engined and highly tuned tractors often draw the spectators' eyes away from the technology of the sledge and its ability to easily control the most powerful of modified tractors.

As one would expect, the sledges in use today have advanced considerably in terms of technology from the first model built in this country by Tom Osborne in 1977, although their methods of operation remain the same: that is, a weight box travels the length of the sledge, increasing the load on the pulling tractor as the distance along the track increases.

The weight transfer sledge or travelling weight box sledge has become the yardstick by which tractors are compared. With so many different tractor divisions and weight classes and the various types of tracks offering different levels of grip for both tractors and sledge, it is important that the sledge can be set up to suit the pulling conditions on the day. For example, a sledge set to stop tractors at around the 80 metre mark on a track

Its appearance may be that of a lorry trailer, but that is where the similarity stops. The Stone Brothers' Hercules weight transfer sledge has the ability to simulate a dead-weight load of around 100 tons and, as such, is capable of stopping the most powerful of modified tractors.

which grips the sledge pan would, perhaps, allow full pulls for every competitor at the same settings on a greasier track.

To overcome this problem and adjust the sledge to suit both track conditions and tractor power, sledges feature transmissions which control the weight box advancing mechanism. By selecting gears, for example, the sledge operator can send the weight box to the front of the sledge within the first 30 metres of track or have the box travel only halfway down the sledge by the time the tractor has reached the full pull mark. This, combined with adding or removing weight from the box, gives the sledge operator the ability to control every tractor class at a pull.

It is interesting to note that Tom Osborne's original sledge of 1977 is still in use. After changing ownership on more than one occasion, it is in service in Scotland and now bears little resemblance to its original design.

During the 1992 season, there were three sledges sanctioned for competition use in the UK. These were the mini sledge, the Midlands sledge and the Stone Brothers' Hercules sledge. The mini sledge has since been sold to an organisation outside tractor pulling, while the larger Midlands sledge, after two unfortunate breakdowns, is now in the hands of Roger Bichanicz, who is also responsible for replacing the mini sledge for the 1993 season.

The sledge currently in use on the BTPA circuit that stands out above the crowd is Hercules, built and owned by the Stone Brothers of Bridgwater in Somerset, first built in the winter of 1988 and developed over the years to become the number one competition sledge in Britain. Inspected and licensed annually, subject to the rules and regulations laid down by the North American Sledge Operators Association (NASOA), Hercules is sanctioned for use at ETPC Championship events.

Sledge operator Graham Stone spent several seasons working Mike Lawrence's sledge (formerly Tom Osborne's) and decided that a more sophisticated sledge was needed to be able to control the growing number of high-powered modified tractors appearing on the scene. This would also allow the sledge operator's platform to be moved from the front and side mounted positions to the rear of the sledge, increasing operator safety.

With ideas and designs based loosely on the specification of an American sledge, Graham set to work. The leading axle on the sledge is a drive axle salvaged from a Seddon Atkinson lorry and this acts as the ground drive mechanism for the sledge's main nine speed Fuller gearbox used to control the weight box speed. It also allows drive to be transmitted back to the ground wheels from a 350 cubic inch (5.7 litre) V8 Chevrolet engine (located above the pan) and makes the sledge self-propelled, avoiding the need to be towed back to the start line—except where track conditions are particularly boggy. The rear axle is a trailing unit from an HGV trailer and helps to spread the weight of the sledge, easing the lot of the engine when in self-propelled mode.

The Chevrolet engine is fitted with both automatic and manual gearboxes; these operate the self-propelled drive, weight box drive and compressor for the many air-activated clutch and brake systems fitted throughout the sledge.

For the statistically minded, Hercules weighs eleven tons empty and can be loaded up with an additional ten tons of movable weight, in half and one ton pieces, which is estimated to result in a transferred deadweight on the pan, when fully loaded, of close to 100 tons. The weight box alone, in maintaining a strong degree of construction, weighs three tons empty and has three specific start positions at the rear of its chassis. This feature allows Graham to 'balance' the sledge weight over the rear axles at the start of each pull, as the front end of the sledge when on the start line must not exert a downward weight on the pan greater than the weight class being pulled. This is particularly important in the 2400 kg class, as the pan alone weighs 2500 kg and therefore some of this weight needs to be transferred towards the rear of the sledge.

Hercules offers nine basic gearbox ratios for moving the weight box up the frame rails without adjusting the loaded weight. However, with three starting positions for the weight box this means that there are 27 permutations for sending the weight box up the sledge without adjusting ballast in the box. A data panel on the sledge provides pullers with information on how far the sledge must move before the weight box reaches its maximum forward position for each of the three starting positions, in each of the nine gears.

This combination of changing weight box travel speeds and the ability to add and subtract up to ten tons of ballast weight in half ton increments gives Graham the provision to set Hercules to control the most powerful tractors on the most unpredictable of track surfaces. However, for those tractors—usually modified— which still manage to get away, additional weight can be added to the front of the pan, while the jewel in the crown is a set of five diamond-shaped flutes strategically placed in the base of the pan which can be screwed down to further increase friction between the pan and the track.

Currently, Hercules is the only sledge in Europe suitable for road transport without the need for a low loader or transport trailer. Hooked to a tractor unit, the all-up rolling weight of tractor unit and sledge is a mere 30 tons.

Just as there are rules and regulations for pulling tractors, this also applies to sledges. With safety a top priority, sledges are equipped with brakes on the sledge drive axle and the weight box, and there must be provision for the sledge operator to activate a kill switch on the pulling tractor. In the event of a tractor breaking away from the sledge or the driver appearing to lose control, the sledge operator makes progressive use of these three braking systems, which must be applied in a set order to avoid worsening the situation. First, the sledge drive axle must be braked, followed by the weight box and finally the kill switch.

Sledge operator safety was originally low on the list of priorities. Current sledges have operator platforms at the back, larger weight pans and shielding at the front of the pan to prevent high wheel speeds from throwing bits of track over the sledge and its operator.

The mini modified division requires a smaller sledge than the other pulling divisions, but with exactly the same operating principles. With the weight box in its rearward position, it can be seen that the back edge of the pan is raised off the track to allow tractors to get away.

Weights can be added onto the front of the pan to increase friction.

As the sledge is pulled forward, the weight box advances up the sledge's frame rails. With the advancing mechanism driven from the ground wheels, the rate is proportional to both forward speed and distance travelled.

If the kill switch is activated before the weight box braking system is applied, then the resulting sudden deceleration of the pulling tractor can cause the weight box to accelerate quickly up the sledge, towards the tractor and driver. On diesel-fuelled tractors, the kill switch operates a flap ahead of the turbocharger inlet and starves the engine of air. With spark ignition tractors, the kill switch earths out the ignition system and literally kills the engine(s).

Tracks

Prior to competitors and spectators gathering at the pulling track, graders and rollers set to work preparing the track for competition. Any vegetation is removed, along with stones and rubble, to leave a clean soil or clay surface for the tractors to pull on. The track needs to be firm, even, free from mounds and holes, and moist. So, track preparation is the order of the day to provide each competitor with a fair surface on which to get the best from their tractors.

If a track is too dry, dust becomes a problem for everyone involved so watering often takes place in summer. If a track is allowed to get too wet—through bad weather before an event— cement powder is often scattered over it to soak up moisture, but this makes the track very adhesive. It is not uncommon for a track to be sheeted over if weather conditions before and during a pull are unfavourable.

Tracks are seldom less than the maximum permitted length of 100 metres (300 ft) with a 30 metre run-off area at the end. Track width must be no less than 9 metres (30 ft) and the track boundaries must be defined with chalk, while length is usually marked with distance boards every 10 metres. Where points pulls are to take place, the track must not be less than 90 metres in length.

Currently, there are four regularly used tracks in the BTPA's tractor pulling circuit. These are at Great Eccleston in Lancashire, Tingewick in Buckinghamshire, Long Ashton in Avon and Yeovil in Somerset. In addition to these 'regular' tracks, tractor pulling takes place at numerous other venues, often supporting shows such as the Headington and Stockley Steam Fair in Wiltshire.

Once a track has been prepared prior to an event, it must be maintained during pulling. After each tractor has made a pull and while the sledge is being returned to the start line, a grader and roller condition the surface of the track, filling in holes and ruts created by the previous competitor.

Measuring a competitor's attempt used to be carried out with wooden pegs and a tape measure. After the tractor had pulled away from the sledge, a peg was driven into the ground along the front edge of the skid pan to mark where the sledge had stopped.

When the rain starts, the track gets covered. A wet track can give too much wheel spin and not enough grip, and those competitors who made good pulls on a dry track then have an unfair advantage.

With the sledge then returned to the start line, the distance could be measured. This method was relied upon for years, but as competition got closer, it was considered too inaccurate and too slow.

The faster and more accurate method now employed uses infra-red technology. The measuring unit is often set up beyond the end of the track and bounces a beam off a reflective board mounted on the sledge. Each time the sledge is positioned on the start line, a distance reading is taken between the measuring unit and the sledge. After the pull has been made, the sledge-to-measuring-unit distance is re-taken to determine how far the sledge has travelled. This is the length of the pull and is measured to the nearest centimetre, from point to point.

A more accurate system of measuring, which is employed by the NTPA, is that of a five-point prism and laser beam set-up.

The prism is located on the sledge and allows a continuous reading of distance during the pull, unlike the point-to-point infra-red system.

If the tractor and sledge 'weave' from side to side going down the track, the distance from point to point would be the same as if the tractor had travelled in a straight line using the infra-red system. The five-point prism continues to record distance, regardless of sledge position, using all its five faces to give a more accurate distance.

With the sledge set correctly and the track well prepared, those tractors which are evenly matched in power often pull to within a few metres of each other and this is usually within the last 10 metres of the track. When competition is close and the sledge operator lets competitors make full use of the track, this is when

After every pull, the track is conditioned and rolled by tractors and equipment following the sledge, so the pulling surface is similar for each and every competitor.

The Midlands sledge in action. With the weight box in its most forward position, maximum load is applied to the pan to stop the tractor. The rate of advance is set by the sledge operator at the start of each class so every competitor pulls the same load.

Too much tyre tread and a loose track surface can have a negative effect during a pull. Dirt building up in front of the pan adds to the weight being pulled, increasing friction.

(*Above*)
A green flag and green lights on the measuring unit and sledge indicate readiness to pull. When forward speed stops, the driver gets a red flag indicating the end of the pull. The measuring unit – shown here at the end of the track – then records how far the sledge has travelled.

A view from the measuring unit. A red reflective board on top of the sledge is used as a registration point for the measuring device.

tractor pulling is at its most exciting. If everyone gets a full pull, the sledge is set too light; likewise, if the tractors are stopped around the 50 metre mark, the sledge is considered too heavy. It is up to the sledge operator to make a pulling class interesting and exciting for spectators and pullers alike.

Naturally, the winner of the class is the competitor who takes the sledge the furthest distance but it is not necessarily achieved by the tractor with the most engines, or the most power. Having thousands of horsepower available won't do any good if you can't get it through the rear wheels and onto the track, where it's really needed most.

A single full pull—that is, taking the sledge all the way down the track—gives an outright winner. However, if two or more competitors achieve full pulls, then a pull-off takes place. It is not enough for the front of the tractor to reach the end of the track; it was the front of the sledge that was set on the start line, so it must be the front of the sledge that crosses the 100 metre or finish line.

With two or more competitors achieving full pulls, the distance beyond the end of the track does not count. So, the sledge must be re-weighted to make the pull tougher, and only those competitors who make full pulls get the chance to run again to determine a class winner.

4 Pro Stock and Super Stock Tractors

The BTPA's 'stock' tractor divisions are about the nearest you'll find to a standard-looking farm tractor. But beneath the agricultural exterior lurks a highly tuned diesel engine, developed to produce a level of horsepower far in excess of the factory figures that manufacturers achieved—their standard engine blocks being the only reminder that the tractor once worked in a field.

And of the pro stock and super stock divisions currently taking part, it is the former which is most likely to return to its humble beginnings.

Pro stock and super stock tractor divisions have standard farm tractor appearance, but the trained eye can quickly tell them apart by tyre size alone. Super stocks, such as the three-stage turbocharged Running Deere, can use rear tyres with a maximum width of up to 30.5 inches.

A look under the bonnet of a super stock tractor reveals the hardware responsible for the power output. The most noticeable addition is the cluster of turbochargers which not only give these tractors their characteristic high-pitched whistles, but more importantly, generate high boost pressures, often in excess of 150 psi. A close look also reveals a non-standard fuel injection pump.

Smokey Joe was once a super stock tractor, but has now been down-rated to run in the pro stock division. Only one turbocharger is allowed and rear tyre width is restricted to a maximum of 24.5 inches.

(*Above*)
Two-stage turbocharging on the Funky Gibbon. Turbochargers not under the bonnet must be shrouded.

The Nipper's low weight to high power ratio was made possible with the use of three-stage turbocharging. The neatly made inlet manifold shows a water injection system plumbed into the underside. Two rotary injection pumps (other side) mounted nose to nose keep fuel delivery high.

To the trained eye, the stock tractors can be spotted by a quick look at the rear tyres—super stock tractors run 30.5 × 32 inch tyres, while the pro stock tractors can be fitted with a maximum tyre size of 24.5 × 32 inches. Those less familiar with the stock tractor divisions will need to take a look under the bonnet, where the real difference can be found.

Whereas pro stock tractors are restricted to the use of only one turbocharger, albeit of any size, the super stock machines can have up to a maximum of four turbochargers—of any size—arranged to produce three stages of boost pressure. And this is most noticeable when the super stock tractors rev up to build turbocharger boost pressure before leaving the start line—the ferocity of exhaust smoke and the high-pitched whistle made by these machines makes them one of the most exciting classes to watch.

However, super stocks are also the most unreliable and temperamental of pulling tractors as a result of this very high state of tune.

With only two main pulling classes in 1978 from the translated NTPA rule book, tractors were easy to recognise, and due to the relative ease of cobbling up a modified tractor with a combination of engines and transmissions, early super stock tractors were thin on the ground. Among the first of these to appear were Mike Hansard's Lincoln Way, George Lyons' Eltrac Deutz and the Funkies (Dave Parnell, Tim Turner and Tony Bourne) with Funky Gibbon—a Massey Ferguson 590 owned by agricultural contractor Ron Gibbons. These were not equipped with more than one turbocharger like the machines in competition today.

By 1979, the Funkies had added a second turbocharger to the Massey Ferguson 590 and, with engine revs maintained to under 3000 rpm, the tractor proved reliable, producing approximately 240 hp from 50–55 psi boost pressure. The success of this development ultimately led to more tractors using more than one turbocharger on an engine.

For 1980, the Funkies acquired a different tractor—a Massey Ferguson 265. This new tractor was called the Nipper and the team changed its name to the Massey Lads. With all the unnecessary agricultural parts removed, the tractor was rebuilt and equipped with two-stage turbocharging and to make sure enough diesel was burnt, it was fitted with a second injector pump and 'tweaked' to achieve maximum fuel delivery.

Throughout the 1980 season, the Nipper gave 100 per cent reliability, winning 17 out of the 34 events during that season. The tractor also had ten second places, three third, three fourth and one fifth position and was already becoming legendary as a result of consistency and the ability to win. That same year, the Nipper was European super stock champion in the 7000 lb and 9000 lb weight classes.

By 1983, further developments were unfolding in the super stock division. The Massey Lads continued the development of the Nipper, giving it a third turbocharger, which proved a little difficult to keep running. This was new ground. No one in the UK had any experience of turbocharging an engine in this way so it was trial-and-error time for the Lads.

When the Nipper ran, it ran very well, but more often than not, it went bang. Turbochargers were melting due to the speed and pressure created in operation, con-rods were bending under the compression in the cylinders (tests showed that a 41 ton force was required to bend standard con-rods) and for a long time, the tractor struggled to rev freely over 4000 rpm. Camshafts were re-profiled and different size turbochargers were used until the tractor started to run exceptionally well.

Before the Nipper was replaced by the Lads' current tractor Perkoil Express in 1986, it was estimated that its 3.8 litre four-cylinder engine produced around 800 hp with almost 180 psi of boost pressure generated by the three-stage turbocharger and water injection set-up. And to date, the Massey Lads know of no other super stock tractor that has competed with a four-cylinder engine and three-stage turbocharging, as larger capacity six-cylinder engines are the more popular option on which to base a

Perkoil Express replaced the Nipper in 1986 and gave the Massey Lads a larger capacity engine to work on. Four turbochargers feature on this 10.5 litre Perkins V8 engine which is said to produce well in excess of 1000 hp. Inlet and exhaust manifolds are all home-made items.

(*Left*)
Bedfordia's Deere Stalker super stock machine, driven by Chris Lay.

Tim Turner leans hard on the Nipper's throttle. Tyre deflection is partly due to low inflation pressures, but mainly a result of the estimated 800 hp developed from 180 psi of turbocharger boost at around 5000 rpm. From the factory, the standard MF 265 tractor would have barely produced 80 hp at a more leisurely 2200 rpm.

Peter Clarke's JBJ Express left the factory as a standard John Deere 4230 tractor. With a four-turbo set-up, three pressure stages are produced (front two turbos feed the third and fourth units) and the wastegate is set to open only when 200 pounds of boost pressure is generated.

JBJ Express in action. With the front wheels off the ground, all the tractor's weight is transferred onto the rear wheels for maximum traction. Power is estimated at 1500 hp.

stock tractor.

At around the same time in 1983, Mike Hansard took to the track with his super stock machine Holton Traxta. Based on a Ford 9600, it featured three-stage turbocharging, water injection and extensive fuel pump modifications, and for awhile it was hard to beat. Like his earlier Lincoln Way tractor, the Holton Traxta was equipped with technology from Jay Forrester, who sent his American super stock tractor across to Mike so that all the pulling goodies could be removed and re-fitted to his new super stock machine.

Other super stock tractors at that time included Peter Clarke's twin turbocharged Windbush, Bedfordia's Deere Stalker, Western Farm Implements' Mr Sheen, John Cornthwaite's Pulling Pig and the Jones Bros' Smokey Joe II.

There are currently six super stock tractors registered with the BTPA and of those, two are equipped with the maximum 'four turbo' systems. These are the Massey Lads' Perkoil Express and Peter Clarke's JBJ Express. An alcohol-burning super stock tractor has yet to grace the BTPA pulling circuit under UK ownership, be it imported from America or home-built, and these machines are as different again from their diesel-fuelled counterparts.

Alcohol-burning super stock tractors (alky burners) use spark ignition systems, unlike diesel engines which rely on compression to ignite the fuel. Alky burners usually achieve greater power with lower turbocharger boost; they usually turn higher wheel speeds, sound different and do not emit any exhaust smoke (unlike diesel-engined super stocks, known as smokers).

Perkoil Express is based on a Massey Ferguson 2775 tractor, and with its 10.5 litre Perkins V8 640 engine, it has the greatest capacity engine in the British super stock division. But the very nature of the engine—its vee configuration—has made multi-stage turbocharging a little difficult to perfect. The turbochargers are arranged to provide two-stage turbocharging on each bank of four cylinders and this is done by cross-boosting the engine. Exhaust gas coming from the left bank of cylinders drives the first stage turbocharger for the same bank of cylinders. From here, the exhaust gas then drives the second stage turbocharger for the opposite bank of cylinders, and vice-versa.

The system is designed to stop surging; should one side of the V8 engine work harder than the other, the extra exhaust gas pressure produced is used to stimulate the other four cylinders. Boost pressure is also evened out using a balance pipe between the two home-made inlet manifolds. Around 150 psi boost pressure is generated and charge cooling is, as on many other stock tractors, afforded by water injection.

Turbocharging is only part of the recipe in producing maximum power from the stock tractor diesel engines. The fuel system requires development work too. With an oversized diesel injector pump with modified pumping elements, big bore pipe work and big bore injectors, fuel on many of these super stock tractors is burnt at an incredible rate of 1.5 gallons in the time it takes to make a pull—around 12 to 15 seconds.

JBJ Express, a John Deere 4230 tractor owned by Peter Clarke and driven by son Stephen, uses its four turbocharger system to arrive at three pressure stages on its six-cylinder diesel engine. Exhaust gas leaving the engine passes through the first turbocharger, then onto the second after which it is split to drive the last two turbochargers simultaneously. The result is a higher level of boost pressure and is reflected in the use of a waste gate on the inlet manifold, set to open at 200 psi.

The super stock division remains limited in tractor numbers as a result of the expense of maintaining and running such a temperamental machine. Pro stock tractor numbers, however, through their generally higher level of reliability but lower state of tune, have increased in popularity and early super stock tractors such as Smokey Joe II and Deere Experience can now be found competing in a more reliable, de-tuned state, in the pro stock division. Some pro stock tractors also take part in the super stock division, which helps to keep divisional tractor numbers up, assisting the selection of how many tractors can take part at European events.

Pro stock tractors were a natural development from the Farmers division which was introduced to encourage farmers to turn up with their tractors and have a go at pulling the sledge. The idea was that once farmers were bitten by the pulling bug, they would return next time with a more ambitious tractor.

In the 1992 pulling season, 15 tractors were competing at pro stock level, the majority based on Fordson Major tractors. Over the years, this has proved to be a popular donor tractor among competitors as parts are easily found and relatively inexpensive. However, tractors such as Never A Nuff (BMC Nuffield), Red Baron (International Harvester), Deere Experience Too (John Deere), French Connection (Renault), Smokey Joe (Ford), Hit 'n' Miss and Overlander (both Massey Ferguson) add variety and excitement to the pro stock tractor pulling division. Interestingly, the pro stock tractor Uphill Struggle (Deutz) is the original Eltrac Deutz which appeared at the first 1978 Royal Show pull.

At pro stock level, tractors are allowed the use of only one turbocharger, one injector pump and only diesel as the fuel, so squeezing power from these machines has become quite an art form. In addition to modifying the diesel injection system and using water injection or heat exchangers for charge cooling, these tractors are often subjected to camshaft changes with radical profiles and wild timing. In a similar fashion to tuning a car engine, the pro stock tractors often have increased valve lift and duration, gas-flowed cylinder heads with bigger valves, polished ports and home-made manifolds with the minimum restriction on gas flow.

With the use of a steel flywheel and clutch assembly and a

(*Left*)
Pro stock tractor French Connection has fuel delivery via a high capacity injection pump. Fuel shut-off linkage runs up to the driver platform for easy access. As engine revs exceed 3000 rpm, a shatter blanket (bottom right-hand corner of photo) must cover the bell housing to protect the driver and spectators from the effects of an exploding clutch/flywheel assembly. The latter must be of steel construction with specific tensile properties.

(*Below*)
Pro stock tractor Uphill Struggle, the Deutz D 8006 owned by Robert Uphill, is said to be the original Eltrac Deutz which appeared at the first British tractor pull.

Lackham Ballistic is one of several tractors governed – by choice –
to the 3000 rpm limit to avoid the cost of fitting a steel
clutch/flywheel assembly and a shatter blanket.

shatter blanket as defined in the rule book, engine speed is only limited by how far the throttle is pushed. It is reported that some NTPA pro stock tractors generate almost 100 psi boost pressure and rev to around 6000 rpm.

However, without the required safety components, engine speed must be governed to a maximum of 3000 rpm. Examples of this type of pro stock tractor are Lackham Ballistic, run by students and lecturer Dick Hanraads from Lackham College of Agriculture, and Hill Billy, owned by Philip Jones. Both are Fordson Major-based machines.

Pro stock tractors generally run standard transmissions and rear axles, and tractors such as Massey Ferguson and Ford with their two-speed change-on-the-move transmissions allow pullers to start off in a low gear, change up to build speed, then change down as the load increases to keep engine speed and turbo boost up, without using the clutch.

Standard single plate clutches are prone to rapid failure, being designed for factory power outputs of around 100 hp to 150 hp from a six-cylinder diesel engine, depending on the model, not the 500 hp to 600 hp more commonly achieved by pro stock tractors, so power transmission is often strengthened with multi-plate or slipper clutches.

Modified Tractors

Modified tractors have long been the most straightforward to build and therefore the most popular division in British tractor pulling since the sport's introduction. However, to remain competitive in the present day, modified tractors are now undoubtedly the most expensive and powerful pulling tractors on the BTPA circuit.

One of the biggest impacts made in the modified pulling division was the introduction of Snoopy, built in 1979 by Mick Cushing. It was the first modified British tractor to use an aircraft engine as its power unit and as such was considered years ahead of its time.

Snoopy was powered by a 40 litre Packard engine and produced 1500 hp, which was far in excess of any other modified tractor competing at that time. Sledge operators struggled to control the power of the tractor and as long as the tractor could start, the modified division was very much a one-horse race. However, it was not long before other pullers adopted the same approach to the modified division, building tractors with unconventional engines. Records show that Snoopy won the 12,000 lb BTPA modified weight class (latterly the 5700 kg and now 5400 kg class) in 1979 and 1980; the 12,000 lb European championship in 1979; and the European indoor championship in 1980 and 1981.

Since being built, Snoopy has changed hands twice, and it can still be found on the track. At the hands of the Whittingham family, Snoopy again won the 12,000 lb modified at the European championship in 1986. The tractor's chassis was then altered to remove weight and allow the Whittinghams to compete with Snoopy in the lighter 9000 lb weight class, which proved unsuccessful. Subsequently, the Whittinghams used the same Packard engine in building Hooker, which has since been sold and now competes as Short Circuit, owned by Julian Leese.

Prior to a rule book being laid down, a modified tractor was recognised as any combination of engine, transmission and rear axle that could fit together and operate, so it was relatively easy for interested parties to build a modified pulling tractor from whatever components could be found. The current rule book

Mick Cushing's Snoopy was the first modified British tractor to use an aircraft engine and as such, was considered years ahead of its time when it appeared in 1979.

defines a modified tractor as any vehicle using any combination of engine(s), transmission(s) and final drive, which must not extend more than 4.26 m forward of the centreline of the rear axle. Tyre size, like the super stock division, is a maximum of 30.5 × 32 inches.

This relative ease of building a modified tractor was reflected in the speed with which many 'new' tractors appeared at pulls. By 1980, there were a significant number of competitors in the modified division, including, in the 7000 lb class, Harold Hewitt's Primrose Perkins, John Heathers' Scrounger and Ken Richardson's Bushy Blower. The heavier 9000 lb and 12,000 lb classes featured Brian Armistead with Moss House Marauder and Ken Smith with Lancashire Lady.

After the chassis died, the engine lived on. Snoopy's 40 litre Packard engine provides the power for Julian Leese's Short Circuit.

Early modified tractors used diesel engines for their power. Here, top-hatted John Heathers prepares to move Scrounger away from the sledge so his pull can be measured.

A late version of Ken Smith's modified tractor Lancashire Lady. Earlier versions of the tractor featured Cummins, then Rolls-Royce power, before settling on the Chevrolet engines.

Because of their large cubic capacities in commercial vehicles, diesel engines were a popular choice for pullers wanting to build powerful modified tractors. Black Queen owned by Simon Harpley was powered by a Perkins V8 510 (8.3 litre) turbocharged diesel engine, as was Harold Hewitt's Primrose Perkins, Kevan Whittingham's Scorton Firefly and Chris Taylor and Alan Entwhistle's Pennine Prowler. And tractors such as Paul Whittingham's Scorton Scorcher and PA & EA Ward's Flying Dragon used twin Perkins V8 510 engines, with turbochargers.

Mike Lawrence's Heavy Hauler modified tractor was also powered by a commercial diesel engine from a Scania truck, while Commer two-stroke diesel engines were used to power Bushy Blower.

Jaguar V12 and Rover V8 car engines were also a popular choice of engine for modified tractors. As a proven power unit, they were easy to tune up and, being lightweight engines with good power outputs, were popular for multi-engined tractor designs, although some pullers were experimenting with engines from alternative vehicles. Terry Barnsley's Whirlwind, for example, was powered by an Alvis Leonides helicopter engine offering 19 litres capacity and 14 cylinders, while Bluebeard, owned by Richard Simmen and Leroy Collis, was powered by a Napier Gazelle gas turbine engine.

Currently only two turbine-engined tractors compete within the BTPA—Satan's Toy, which is a 900 kg mini tractor, and Avon Lady, owned by Chris George, which is powered by an Armstrong Siddeley Mamba engine more commonly found in Fairey Gannet naval reconnaissance aircraft. Estimated to produce 1400 shaft horsepower at 15,000 rpm, the Mamba engine in Avon Lady is started by a donkey engine which spins the gas turbine up to 5000 rpm before its own starting procedure can commence. The tractor is spectacular to watch, but with a fixed speed engine is said to be difficult to control.

The gas turbine-powered Avon Lady is Chris George's second tractor, following on from the twin V8-engined original Avon Lady built in 1979 by Chris George and Chris Keel.

In the early 1980s, diesel-engined modified tractors proved to be short of controllable power. The use of multi-stage turbocharging meant that all the power was either 'on' or 'off', and if the tractor looked to be heading out of bounds, it was difficult to throttle off a diesel engine, straighten the tractor and then re-apply the power, without loosing precious turbocharger boost. So it followed that pullers needed more flexible engines with greater power outputs. And it was soon to unfold that the cheque book was to play an influencing role in deciding which tractors would sit at the top of the tree.

In the winter of 1982, Dave Prince built Euro Invader powered by a V12 Rolls-Royce 27-litre Meteor engine (ex-tank) running on aviation and methanol fuels and was powerful enough to gain second and third places in the European championships of 1986 and 1987 respectively (the tractor still competes, now as Old Ironsides owned by William Rosewell).

Rolls-Royce Griffon engines soon followed, and by 1985 a race began to get the first Griffon-engined tractor onto the track. Mike Lawrence had progressed from his diesel-powered Heavy Hauler to the single Griffon-engined Chariot of Fire I and Brian Armistead had built his first Griffon-engined tractor, Desperate Dan Mk I, to replace the Jaguar-engined Moss House Marauder.

These 36.7 litre V12 engines with four valves per cylinder were more at home in Shackleton aircraft (aero Griffon specification) and motor torpedo boats (sea Griffon specification) than tractors,

SAM 2 powered by a Perkins V8 510 engine.

Walter Parkinson's Bits & Pieces was powered by an AEC Mandator V8 diesel engine. Note the use of dual wheels, which were banned in the mid-eighties after many parted company with their tractor during pulls.

(*Below*)
Desperado was powered by an experimental V8 Jaguar engine and used an automatic transmission.

Scorton Firefly in action. Owned by Kevan Whittingham, the tractor used a Perkins V8 510 engine and filled the sledge operator's lungs with smoke. The sledge belonged to Stan Cookson and the operator sat with his back to the tractor at the high end of the sledge.

Bluebeard used a Napier Gazelle gas turbine engine.

but with 2435 hp at a low 2750 rpm, it seemed that for the time being, there was plenty of pulling power for the modified tractor division. The sea Griffon engine chosen by Brian Armistead, when installed in a boat, was equipped with an output shaft at the rear of the engine, leading to a gearbox which eased its installation into a tractor, unlike the aero Griffon which had a contra-rotating propellor driven from the front of the engine. Interestingly enough, both tractors made their pulling debuts at a very wet Norfolk track in June.

During the 1985 season, the power of the Griffon engine was fully realised by Mike Lawrence in Chariot of Fire I in its first season but the tractor suffered a number of breakages. Gearbox shafts, rear axle hub reduction and pinion shafts were repeatedly broken, each time replaced by a bigger and stronger component, until a satisfactory level of reliability was achieved.

In 1987, Dave Prince's Euro Invader had become outpowered so, after considering the options of building and buying, he opted for the latter and bought a tractor equipped with two 28 litre V12 Allison engines from the US—Allison engines, like Rolls-Royce Griffon engines, were more commonly found in American fighter aircraft from around the 1940s and 1950s. The tractor, known

Whirlwind being towed back after a pull. Power was via a 14 cylinder Alvis Leonides helicopter engine.

Chris George's first version of Avon Lady, powered by two 6.6 litre International V8 engines running on aviation fuel.

as El Toro, was acquired from Wayne Longnecker of Iowa and was equipped with methanol injection, but by the time the tractor arrived in Britain in January 1988, it was downrated to run on petrol and fitted with smaller superchargers to allow Dave to develop the tractor at his own pace.

Renamed Atlantic Invader, the tractor performed well, but was sold in favour of another twin Allison-engined tractor, which Dave currently runs, known as Just Another Invader. Its Allison engines are mounted one behind the other, with the rear engine slightly higher than the front (a configuration known as 'stair-stepped'), which allows the rear engine to be removed so the tractor can take part in the lightest, 2400 kg modified weight class. Stair-stepping has appeared with numerous engine types, but not yet with the higher capacity Griffon engines. It is, perhaps, just a matter of time before a stair-stepped Griffon-engined tractor joins the circuit.

(*Above*)
Mike Lawrence's
diesel-powered Heavy
Hauler.

(*Below*)
The succession of Brian Armistead's Desperate Dan tractors
started with the Rolls-Royce Griffon-engined Dan Mark 1.

(*Left*)
Jim Snell's first Starlight
Express tractor used
only a few Jaguar
engines. A single V12
unit was enveloped by
eight six-cylinder
engines. Starlight
Express is shown here
with the front two
engines removed to
qualify for a lighter
weight class.

The current version of Avon Lady uses an Armstrong Siddeley Mamba turbine engine.

Things can – and do – go wrong for many pullers.

(*Right*)
The Whittinghams' Snoopy suffered a supercharger explosion on one of its Griffon engines.

(*Below*)
Snoopy's exploded supercharger.

Atlantic Invader is currently owned by Jim Snell, who now runs the tractor as Starlight Express II, complete with methanol injection and manually operated, not slipper type, clutches. The tractor is a completely different animal from Jim's previous machine, the spectacularly powered Starlight Express I which used one V12 and eight straight-six Jaguar engines in its final form.

To date, the popularity of Griffon and Allison engines is reflected in the growing number of tractors using these power units in the modified pulling division. Both Mike Lawrence and Kevan Whittingham use twin Griffon engines mounted side by side in their tractors Chariot of Fire II and Snoopy.

Unlike many pullers who opt to build their own chassis for tractors or to import complete tractors, Mike Lawrence built Chariot of Fire II using an Engler chassis (designed and built by American tractor puller Tim Engler). Other tractors are on the European circuit with Engler chassis but have appeared as complete machines, imported 'ready to pull'. According to Mike, his is the only tractor *built* in Europe with such a chassis. And Mike reckons that an Engler chassis is often copied, but never bettered.

Just Another Invader, owned by Dave Prince, is powered by two Allison V12 engines, which are mounted on the chassis in a 'stair-stepped' configuration. This allows the rear engine to be removed in a matter of minutes and the tractor then competes in the lighter 2400 kg class. The tractor has since been fitted with a methanol fuel injection system on the front engine.

Black Gold, owned by Ashley Middleton, was imported from Canada during 1992 and is a single Allison-engined tractor. With two stage supercharging and a methanol fuel injection system, it is estimated that the tractor develops almost 3000 hp.

A growing number of pullers have imported twin and single Allison-engined tractors from America. Jim Snell and Dave Prince have twin Allison-engined tractors, whereas Ashley Middleton's Black Gold only has one Allison engine.

Brian Armistead's first Griffon-engined tractor Desperate Dan Mk 1 was replaced by a Mk 2 model with considerable engine modifications. This 'new' Desperate Dan was to give Brian more power with its twin-turbocharged and methanol-injected Griffon engine. However, a Griffon engine had not previously been tuned to such a state, and the tractor became recognised as a fire hazard at the many pulls it attended. After a fairly unsuccessful run, Brian, like other tractor pullers, looked overseas for a more powerful tractor, and in 1990 Desperate Dan Mk 3 appeared.

This ex-Pat Freels tractor (known in America as Dollar Devil) is Brian's current machine and is fitted with five very expensive and very powerful (some say 1500 hp per engine) supercharged V8, methanol-injected Chevrolet engines, one of which can be removed to allow the tractor to compete in the 3400 kg class. Having unfortunately blown up many engines in the last few seasons, Brian is also recognised as having the most valuable pile of scrap engine components in the country. But that, as they say, is tractor pulling.

Chevrolet engines are becoming a popular choice of engine for modified tractors. Brian Armistead's present Desperate Dan tractor runs five supercharged and methanol-injected Chevrolet V8 engines.

Modified tractors were easy to build, linking numerous engines together in search of power. Here, two pairs of Jaguar engines are first linked crank-to-crank and then power is transmitted through a crossbox to the rear axle.

6

900 kg Mini Modified Tractors

Since the public appearance of the first mini pullers in the UK at the Town and Country Festival during the August Bank Holiday weekend in 1985, this class has grown steadily to include 11 tractors in 1992, and others are expected to surface over the next few years. The compact size and relatively low level of technology—compared to modified tractors—makes mini tractors appealing to the sport's newcomers.

Being only 900 kg in weight, these mini modified tractors can be easily transported via trailers behind a large car or four-wheel drive vehicle, whereas larger pulling tractors often require upwards of a 7.5 tonne truck or converted coach as an effective means of transportation.

An early version of Hurtmore Horror (then with only one Rover V8 engine) pulling Paul Haylock's twin-axled sledge.

The United States' NTPA mini regulations allow the use of one engine up to a maximum capacity of 575 cubic inches (9.4 litres) when supercharged, increasing to 650 cubic inches (10.6 litres) maximum when naturally aspirated. NTPA mini weight is 1800 lb (818 kg). BTPA regulations have not yet implemented a limit on engine size and number of them allowed. The only limit is a maximum tractor weight of 900 kg, introduced in 1987.

The mini modified tractor division was introduced by the NTPA in 1974, then with weight classes of 1500 lb and 1700 lb (681 kg and 772 kg), but a tractor of this type had yet to be seen on the UK circuit. At an indoor tractor pull at Membury airfield around Easter 1982, Gordon Whitefield from Andover unveiled the first British-built mini modified tractor. Blue Mover, as the tractor was named, featured a 351 cubic inch (5.7 litre) Ford V8 engine, C3 Ford automatic transmission and a Ford 60 series rear axle.

At the same time, there was talk of a sledge being built, but as this didn't materialise, Gordon—with a tractor but no sledge to pull—decided to build a mini sledge. Over the winter of 1983/84, he set about building a scaled-down version of Tom Osborne's sledge so that he would at least have something to pull. At the same time, husband and wife team Rod and Kim Harrison from Cambridgeshire expressed such an interest in Blue Mover that the tractor was sold on, and this left Gordon with more time to concentrate on sledge operation.

By the time the Town and Country Festival came round in 1985, Gordon's sledge was ready for use with the only two mini tractors in the country, both owned by the Harrisons. Rod's tractor, called Stardust, was powered by a 7 litre V8 Pontiac engine, while Kim drove Playgirl, the former Blue Mover.

At the start of the following season, mini pulling went to the Lincolnshire Showground and the class had doubled in size: Ted Corner and the Hurtmoor Horror tractor pulling team and Andy Waygood turned up with their mini tractors. In that same season, a growing interest in mini pulling saw the introduction of several more tractors and an additional sledge built by Paul Haylock. A fifth tractor had been built by Guy Wevell, but in its final stages of preparation it suffered a fire which delayed its introduction.

The Haylock sledge, unlike Gordon's version, featured twin axles and was relatively long to start with. In time, its length was shortened. This changed the operating characteristics of the sledge dramatically and led to light-hearted competition between the sledge operators.

It was not until Steve and Peter Cox introduced their mini tractor G-Force that attention really turned to the maximum allowable tractor weight of 900 kg. Around this time, the majority of mini tractors, with the exception of G-Force, exceeded the maximum permitted class weight limit, which gave a definite traction advantage over the Coxes' tractor. To ban the majority of minis from pulling because of the apparent weight problem would

Like larger modified tractors, the 900 kg mini tractors feature a wide variety of engines. Milford Lady has a flat-six continental engine, more commonly found in self-propelled field guns. It is also turbocharged.

have prevented this pulling division from reaching its current status and would also have eliminated the division from qualifying for entry to a European championship, so it was decided to let the remaining heavier tractors take part, with the provision that weight-saving materials such as aluminium would be implemented into mini tractor design to cut down on weight without sacrificing strength. This was exploited and continued for almost two seasons.

During these early days of mini pulling, the class weight at 900 kg provided no allowance for the weight of safety equipment. Shatter blankets were not made a statutory requirement until 1987 so a protective steel housing which completely shrouded the bell housing had to be fitted and this gave a considerable increase in tractor weight.

In 1987, with continued interest in the 900 kg mini pullers, the decision was made to form the MPC GB (Mini Pullers Club, Great Britain). Ted Corner was appointed chairman and the MPC held its first club pull at Shackleford, Surrey, in the autumn of 1987.

As chairman of the mini pullers club, Ted tried hard to prevent 'cheque book pulling' from taking over the development of the mini tractors. He reasoned that if restrictions were implemented

Groundhog, owned by Mark Burton, was originally Rod Harrison's Stardust tractor and features 7 litre Pontiac power. The tractor is shown here pulling Gordon Whitefield's sledge.

The 900 kg mini modified tractor division is a low cost and simple alternative to the larger modified tractor division. Minis must not exceed 1.83 m in width and 2.44 m in length, the latter being measured from the centre of the rear axle.

A single V12 Jaguar engine is used to power Stray Cat.

(*Below*)
Symphony for the Devil also uses Jaguar V12 power, but with the addition of two superchargers and fuel injection.

on maximum engine size, number of turbochargers and super-chargers, the 900 kg mini tractors would appeal to a wide audience and encourage the introduction of more tractors and competitors. To date, such mechanical restrictions are not yet in force and the MPC has, in readiness, made provision to sub-divide its competitors into A and B classes to try to balance out the competition: the top 50 per cent of the MPC would pull in A class and the bottom 50 per cent would then pull in B class. Then, for example, at the end of each season, the top two tractors in B class would move up to A and the bottom two tractors from A class move down to B.

1987 was also the year when the NTPA wanted to reduce the weight of UK and European mini tractors to 800 kg, to bring all mini divisions into line on a common weight class. Strong opposition from the MPC via the BTPA and the European mini pullers saw this rejected and the class remained at 900 kg. Pullers were having enough trouble keeping chassis of mini tractors with powerful V8 engines in one piece as it was, and to reduce tractor weight further would only add to this

Too much wheel speed in far from ideal track conditions.

problem. Currently, the NTPA's mini division competes at 818 kg (1800 lb).

Politics and disputes, it seems, creep into just about everything and the mini pullers club was no exception as sledge ownership received a good shake up in 1987. With a pull scheduled at Rod and Kim Harrison's in Cambridgeshire, Gordon Whitefield had loaded up his sledge and was ready to head up-country to the event when disaster struck and the crankshaft broke within his truck's engine. A replacement sledge was required to enable the pull to go ahead, and as Paul Haylock's twin axled sledge was the only one available, it was the second choice. But friction between the Haylock and the Harrison families meant that there was no way that Paul Haylock would take his sledge to the event. Time was ticking away and drastic measures had to be taken. It seemed that the only option remaining was for someone to step in and buy the sledge. And so it happened that Ken Richardson bought the sledge to make sure that the pull went ahead. Strangely enough, following this event, the sledge was rarely used again, although it is understood that it is set to return to the track during the 1993 season in a revised and refurbished form, replacing the mini sledge sold by the Chapmans at the end of the 1992 season.

Gordon Whitefield's sledge has changed ownership too and resulted in his retirement from the sport. In the hands of father and son team Brian and Mark Chapman, the original mini sledge was subjected to major surgery. Its chassis was shortened and the nose end lowered to improve its characteristics; this enabled the sledge to be transported on a beaver-tailed truck rather than towed. The sledge was also equipped with a larger pan.

Ted Corner was active in the position of MPC GB chairman until the end of the 1992 season, when Northants mini puller Mark Pacey took over.

In the ETPC rule book, mini pullers are defined as any tractor without a standard engine block or crankcase for the type of chassis in which the engine is mounted. So, providing that the tractor including fuel, oil and driver does not exceed 900 kg in weight, 1.83 m in width and 2.44 m in length (the latter is the maximum distance forward from the centre line of the rear axle), any combination of engine, transmission and rear axle can be used to build such a machine, unless otherwise stipulated. In terms of component shielding and safety requirements, the mini tractor is to meet the criteria laid down for the larger modified tractor division.

Because of tractor size, power for the 900 kg mini tractor division is predominantly from single V8 petrol engines of varying capacities, although that is not to say that other engines or multiples of engines cannot be used. Satan's Toy owned by brothers Neal and Nigel Davis, for example, is currently the only UK mini tractor powered by a gas turbine engine. Its Rolls-Royce Gnome power unit is rated at 1200 hp and makes for some lively,

Two Rover V8 engines for Ted Corner's Hurtmore Horror.

to say the least, if not a little uncontrollable, tractor pulling.

Milford Lady, originally built by Mick Whitnell and now owned by Alan Shepherd, is another tractor which features an engine of a different sort. Its six-cylinder horizontally opposed, air-cooled continental engine—more commonly found in self-propelled field guns—has been turbocharged and runs on a mixture of avgas and methanol and adds to the excitement of the mini tractor division which features tractors of incredible power to weight ratios.

Ted Corner's Hurtmoor Horror was, in its early days of using only one 3.5 litre Rover V8 engine, subjected to methanol injection in the search for more power, but this has since been shelved in favour of using two 3.5 litre Rover V8 engines. Both engines have undergone camshaft changes and cylinder head modifications, and their estimated power outputs of over 300 hp per engine have given rise to chassis problems, now identified and dealt with.

A wild ride with Satan's Toy. A Rolls-Royce Gnome turbine engine has 1200 hp on tap and some say if the tractor had rotor blades, it might fly.

Pulling for Points

Not long after the start of British tractor pulling, when the sport was beginning to establish a pulling circuit and there was a fast-growing membership with competing tractors, a system for allocating points to competitors was introduced. This was made applicable to each weight class within the pulling divisions, so that end-of-season champions could be determined. The points allocation system is one of the few introductions that have altered only slightly over the years.

The top ten positions in each class are awarded scores. Those events allocated as points pulls are recognised as championship rounds, and at the end of the season, the points accumulated determine which puller becomes British Champion in each class—the total number of points pulls which take place each season being determined after the season's events list has been finalised.

In the current points allocation system, any competitor able to hook onto the sledge receives 5 points, and position points are awarded as follows:

Winner	30 points	(25 plus 5 hook points)
Second place	27 points	(22 plus 5 hook points)
Third place	24 points	(19 plus 5 hook points)
Fourth place	21 points	(16 plus 5 hook points)
Fifth place	19 points	(14 plus 5 hook points)
Sixth place	17 points	(12 plus 5 hook points)
Seventh place	15 points	(10 plus 5 hook points)
Eighth place	13 points	(8 plus 5 hook points)
Ninth place	11 points	(6 plus 5 hook points)
Tenth place	9 points	(4 plus 5 hook points)

In earlier years points were awarded to the top ten positions in each division where applicable, as some pulling divisions and weight classes did not have enough tractors to fill these ten positions. Points awarded were 10 for first place, descending by 1 point for remaining competitors. Hook points were not given.

The points allocation system for mini modified tractors is slightly different. To encourage participation in every event, competitors are awarded 5 additional points for simply turning

Along with the points go the trophies. The tractors are Woodhall Warrior, followed by Hardwick Beast.

up and taking part. A win, therefore, can result in 35, not 30 points: 25 for first place plus 5 hook points and 5 additional points for effort and participation. At the end of the season, this can make a significant difference to a competitor's total, and the system is said to prevent pullers from 'saving' their tractors solely for more important points pulls.

If bad weather prevents competition at a points pull, then those tractors registered for taking part in each class affected are awarded an equal amount of points, the value of which is determined by dividing the total number of points possible between the number of tractors taking part.

During general competition, the first puller in each class is designated test puller, and the head track marshall and the sledge operator use this first attempt to determine whether the sledge is correctly set for competition. If the sledge needs further adjustment, the second puller is then designated the test puller, and the previous competitor drops six positions before returning to pull. Where there are fewer than six tractors taking part, the test puller goes last.

When the sledge is set, the test puller is given the option of accepting that test pull as a measured pull, or of taking a second attempt later in the class. The decision to take a second bite at the cherry automatically discounts the first pull and prevents test pullers from trying again and then selecting the best of two attempts.

With title points at stake, pullers try harder to win. Here, Mike Hansard's Lincoln Way has its sights firmly set on the top end of the track.

A good start is everything in tractor pulling. Here, Mike Simmons glances quickly at the instruments as he leaves the start line, to see if Hit 'n' Miss is performing as expected. At this point, if pullers are not entirely satisfied with the way their pull is going, they can attempt to stop before the 20 m line and qualify for an immediate, and final, re-pull.

In addition to the points awarded to the top ten tractors in each weight class, hook points are also allocated to those tractors that make it to the sledge.

The first competitor in each class is designated test puller and if the sledge is deemed set after this test pull, that competitor has the option of accepting the pull or dropping six places before trying again.

Depending on the weather and the track, pulling conditions can vary considerably from the start of a class to the finish, so being test puller can have its advantages. In the time the second to fifth tractors take to pull, track conditions can have dried out more. This can be beneficial to modified and super stock tractors with high wheel speeds, relying on friction between tyre and track for the best grip. Although too dry a track can give too much wheel slip and tractors struggle to get moving off the start line. Pro stocks run slower wheel speeds and can suffer too much wheel slip on too dry a surface when the weight is transferred onto the tractor. So, a test puller can watch preceding competitors' efforts and try to 'read' the track to see which parts/side of the track holds more grip and a smooth ride—too much tractor bounce can 'lift' weight from the driving wheels slowing forward speed and reducing grip. There are also disadvantages: the track condition may have deteriorated, and the very nature of tractor pulling means that a second pull can be just enough to result in a breakdown on the track, in which case the puller only receives hook points.

When competition is in progress, pullers often watch each other to see how the track performs. They can then spot the position of the sledge at the start line to suit their pull. Once a tractor is hooked to the sledge, competitors must take up the strain—no jerking is allowed—and make an honest attempt to pull the sledge.

If a puller cannot move the sledge past the white flags at the 20 metre mark, or if a puller is not happy with the way the

Two flagmen are responsible for competitors when on the track. Using their flags, they signal to the competitor when the measuring unit and sledge are ready to go. To commence pulling under a red flag will result in disqualification.

tractor is running before passing the white flags and shows an intention to stop, an immediate second attempt is allowed. The sledge is returned to the start line either under its own power or with a tow-back tractor, and the measuring unit is reset. Then comes the puller's final chance to make a measured pull, and whatever distance is achieved, from 0 to a full pull, it counts as a measured pull.

This first 20 metres of track is where the pulling strategies often unfold. Competitors must pay close attention to how their tractors perform off the line. Is engine rpm—and turbo boost pressure, where applicable—up where it should be? Are the front wheels off the ground, balancing all the tractor's weight on the rear axle for maximum traction? Is the tractor pulling in a straight line? These factors can determine whether or not a puller will show intention to stop before the white flags and then qualify for an immediate repull.

While pullers are on the track, they are under the control of two flagmen: one at the start line, who is responsible for the readiness of track, sledge and puller, and a second, who takes a position near the 100 metre mark and is responsible for the balance of the course. It is up to the flagmen to keep the puller under a red flag until the measuring unit and sledge are ready. Flashing green and red beacons on the sledge are used to indicate status, and when the signal is given by the flagmen, the puller then has three minutes to make a pull.

While on the track, pullers can be disqualified for a number of reasons, in which case they forfeit the right to any points in that class unless in a pull-off. Two of the most common reasons for disqualification are crossing the trackside boundary while pulling and dropping ballast weights on the track. Both result in an instant red flag. Other causes for disqualification include leaving the start line under a red flag, use of illegal fuels (such as nitromethane, nitrous oxide, combustion accelerators and other oxygen carriers), loss of safety equipment, failure of safety equipment to operate under a green flag and the use of illegal equipment.

Should a competitor be disqualified during a pull-off, points are awarded for last place in a pull-off. For example, if there are three competitors in a pull-off, the disqualified competitor is awarded points for third place.

At the end of a pull, the tractor must be able to back up to the sledge to allow the hook and safety connections to be disengaged and then to drive away from the sledge under its own power. Failure to do so can, at the discretion of the flagmen, result in a disqualification.

Tow-back tractors are positioned at the end of the track so that pullers can be towed back to either the pull-off area or pit area, saving their highly tuned engines for the next run. This is particularly applicable to the modified tractor division.

Every puller has his sights set on a full pull and the throttle is set to 'kill' the moment the wheels start to move. A class win is worth 30 points for all but the 900 kg mini tractors.

At the start of each pull, competitors get the chance to 'spot' the position of the sledge on the start line in search for the better parts of the track. Here David Powell has opted to take Little Willie down the left-hand side of the track.

Above)
Competitors can enter their vehicles once in each weight class, subject, of course, to tractor weight being under the permitted maximum for that class. Pro stock and super stock tractors must carry a minimum of 100 kg of movable ballast.

One of the most consistent pro stock tractors in recent years has been Major Tom. Here, Gary Dunn reels in yet another full pull as this old Fordson Major, showing no signs of giving up, digs hard into the surface of the track aiming to haul the sledge way beyond the finish line.

The European Connection

The European Tractor Pulling Committee (ETPC), based in the Netherlands, was formed in 1987, and Jan Buitenhuis is currently president. It is a coordinating body with the objective of promoting tractor pulling in the widest possible way throughout Europe.

Thirteen tractor pulling organisations from twelve countries in Europe are affiliated to the ETPC as follows:

Belgische Kracht Tractoren Vereniging (BKTV) **Belgium**
British Tractor Pullers Association (BTPA) **Britain**
Dansk Tractor Treak (DTT) **Denmark**
Deutsche Trecker Trek Organisation (DTTO) **Germany**
Federation Francaise des Tracteur Pulling (FFTP) **France**
Finnish Tractor Pullers Association (FTPA) **Finland**
Letzeburger Trecker Treck Organisation (LTTO) **Luxembourg**
Nederlandse Trekker Trek Organisatie (NTTO) **Netherlands**
Norgen Tractor Pulling Kommittee (NTPK) **Norway**
Ostereichische Tractor Pulling Organisation (OTPO) **Austria**
Ostereichische Trecker Treck Organisation (OTTO) **Austria**
Schweizer Trecker Treck Vereinigung (STTV) **Switzerland**
Svenska Tractor Pulling Kommiten (STPK) **Sweden**

In addition to the modified, super stock, mini and pro stock pulling divisions, which take part at BTPA events, the ETPC also sanctions a two-wheel drive pulling division in 2600 kg and 2900 kg weight classes. Such a division operates within the NTTO.

Every year, the tractor pulling season culminates with a two-day European championship event, which is hosted by a different member country each year. The top tractors from the ETPC's affiliated organisations participate to determine the European champions for each pulling division's weight class.

For many pullers, this is the icing on the cake, as tractors are usually selected to attend the ETPC's annual showcase event on the strength of the season's performance. The number of tractors permitted to attend from each affiliated country is determined by the ETPC, based on a percentage figure calculated on the total number of tractors registered in each country.

It is a system said to maintain tractor quality, not quantity, at

The ETPC also sanctions a two-wheel drive truck division, in addition to the more usual stock and modified tractor division. Rattle 'n' Hum, a Dutch machine, makes a guest appearance on British soil.

a European championship and the selection process has, in the past, carried a limit of no more than four tractors in any one class from any one country. The previous year's champions, of course, are automatically selected to defend their titles.

As a European championship is held over two days, there is usually the provision to run a modified class long into the night, when these tractors become even more exciting to watch. The combination of exotic fuels such as alcohol and methanol with highly tuned engines results in a stunning display of fire, as shimmering exhaust heat seen during the day is transformed into a multi-coloured flame show during the night.

Unlike a standard BTPA event which allows pullers only one chance to make a measured pull (with an immediate re-pull after attempting to stop before the white flags at 20 metres), a European championship operates a system whereby each competitor has two attempts to make a full pull. After all competitors in a class have made their first pulls, the class is then immediately re-run but only includes those pullers who did not make a full pull on their first attempt.

After all competitors in a class have made their second pulls, the sledge is adjusted for the pull-off and only then does the

A European championship event often goes on well into the night, when it illuminates another side of modified pulling. Exotic fuels often light up the sky with a spectacular show of exhaust flames and glowing manifolds. Popeye, a Dutch tractor driven by Jan Van Alphen, is one of a handful of tractors in Europe to run with three Allison V12 engines. This methanol-injected monster produces around 7500 hp.

Museums Killer is one of two modified tractors from the German Kiemele stables, both of which use supercharged Arias V8 engines. Obviously, the emphasis here is on power, although the smaller Museums Cat has only three Arias engines, arranged in a stair-stepped configuration.

(*Above*)
The second flagman at a European championship event must be a member of the ETPC International Jury.

Rustica, a French super stock tractor, in action on home turf during the 1992 European championship event at Bernay, France.

competition get tough. The emphasis here in the early stages is to put on more of a show for the spectators, rather than have too tough a competition. To stop a powerful tractor just as it reaches the full pull marker will result in less powerful machines being stopped within the first 50 m. With the sledge set slightly lighter than usual during the first two attempts, tractors with a power disadvantage then have a better chance of achieving a full pull. However, if the first five tractors in a given class all make full pulls, the class will automatically be re-started, as competition is considered too easy.

In addition to the slight differences in event procedure at a European championship, there are also slight differences in the general rules for the event. The second flagman on the track must be a member of the ETPC international jury and the event must feature six of the most popular classes pulled in Europe plus minis, although this is a rule subject to change at the ETPC's discretion.

The 1992 European championship was organised by the FFTP at Bernay, France, and included all four weight classes of modified tractors, both weight classes in super stock and the 900 kg mini pullers. As the pro stock division operates only

Addiction, the John Deere 4255 super stock tractor being driven here by its former owner, Ron Bultemeier, is bound for the European championship circuit at the hands of its new owner, Thomas Paterson from Sweden.

Starfighter from Denmark features an 18-cylinder rotary engine with one turbocharger for every six cylinders.

within the BTPA in Europe, it is not eligible for inclusion at a European championship.

If tractor breakage occurs on the first pull, providing the tractor has not passed the 20 m mark, that competitor will get a total of two chances. However, if the last tractor in a class experiences mechanical problems, then a time limit of six minutes (at the discretion of the flagmen) is allocated in which that puller must hook up and make an attempt to pull.

In a European championship pull-off situation, pullers are required to take part in the order in which they made full pulls. If the first puller fails to reach the 38 m mark, then the sledge is automatically re-adjusted. However, if the first puller succeeds in making a full pull, then all contestants must pull at that sledge setting unless the track judges rule that the sledge operator has made a mistake in adjusting the sledge.

BTPA members have won a number of championships since the first European event was held at Flevohof, Holland, in 1979. The first British tractor to become a European champion, of course, was Mike Cushing's Snoopy in the 5700 kg modified class. Since then, other British tractors have followed with European championship titles. In 1980, Peter Clarke's Windbush Whistler, a Fordson Super Major with one turbocharger, took the title in the 2400 kg class while in the same year, the Massey Lads' Nipper took both the 3400 kg and 4400 kg super stock

(*Above*)
Chariot of Fire II, owned by Mike Lawrence, was European champion in 1990 in the 4400 kg modified class. The tractor features a Tim Engler chassis and two 36.7 litre Rolls-Royce Griffon engines.

Hurricane, a Ford 9600 super stock, weighted up in the 4400 kg class.

Alan Williams with Limited Edition en-route to winning the 1992 European championship title in the 2400 kg modified class. With a third engine, the tractor also competes in the 3400 kg class.

(*Below*) Jim Snell's twin Allison-engined Starlight Express II is a strong contender for a European championship title. With methanol injection and high speed superchargers on both engines, power output is estimated to be around 5000 hp.

classes and the 4400 kg super stock class again in the following year.

In 1985 and 1986, the twin Jaguar V12-engined Hardwick Beast owned by brothers Brian and David Creed won the 2400 kg modified class. Also in 1986, the remaining three modified classes were also won by British tractors. The 3400 kg modified class went to Alan Williams with Supertramp running with only five of its usual six Rover 3.5 litre V8 engines, the heavier 4400 kg modified class went to Brian Armistead with his first Desperate Dan tractor powered by a single Rolls-Royce Griffon engine, while the top weight 5700 kg modified class went to the original 1979 champion Snoopy, owned then by the Whittingham family and driven by Neil Whittingham.

The following year, Mike Lawrence was to start his run of European championship titles with his Chariot of Fire tractor. Powered by a single Rolls-Royce Griffon engine, Chariot of Fire I took the 5700 kg modified class in 1987 and again in 1989. Taking this latter title, Chariot of Fire I was considerably underpowered compared to the twin Griffon-engined It Kypmantsje and the twin Allison-engined tractors Popeye and Museum Giant.

In 1988, Peter Clarke returned to take his second European championship title, but this time in the 3400 kg super stock class with Running Deere, a three stage turbocharged John Deere 4430 tractor bought from American tractor puller Ron Johnson in the previous year. By 1990, Mike Lawrence had returned with Chariot of Fire II, this time powered by two Rolls-Royce Griffon engines, and won the European title in the 4400 kg modified class that year.

1991 saw the European championship take place at Great Eccleston, near Blackpool, when Brian Armistead became European champion in the 3400 kg modified class with his Chevrolet-powered Desperate Dan tractor while running only four of its five supercharged V8 engines in this lighter weight class. The same year also saw Alan Williams (of Supertramp fame) return for his second European title with the Williams Brothers' latest tractor, Limited Edition, winning the 2400 kg modified class using only two of the tractor's three Chevrolet V8 engines.

And in 1992, at the European championship in Bernay, France, both Brian Armistead and Alan Williams repeated their previous year's victories in the same weight classes to maintain their titles.

Indoor tractor pulling is also a part of tractor pulling in Europe, and Ahoy Stadium in Rotterdam is a favourite venue for tractors of all divisions. With diesel-powered machines, Ahoy Stadium operates a smoke extraction system comprising an umbilical pipe attached to the pulling tractor, via the sledge.

(*Facing page*)
Gary Dunn's pro stock Major Tom in a demonstration pull at the 1991 European championship.

Appendix I
BTPA competitors and licensed vehicles, 1993

Name	Division*	Tractor	County
Armistead, Brian	Mod	Desperate Dan	Lancashire
Bichanicz, David	Mini	Top Cat	Northamptonshire
Bichanicz, David	Mod	Throbbin Robin	Northamptonshire
Bichanicz, Roger	Mod	Alley Cat	Northamptonshire
Broad, Alistair	SS	Running Deere	Cheshire
Brown, Geoff	Mini	Stray Cat	Leicestershire
Bruegger, Tony	TWD	Noddy Truck	Avon
Burton, Mark	Mini	Groundhog	Leicestershire
Clarke, Peter	SS	JBJ Express	Buckinghamshire
Clarke, Stephen	SS	JBJ Express	Buckinghamshire
Corner, Edward	Mini	Hurtmoor Horror	Surrey
Creed, Brian	Mod	Hardwick Beast	Buckinghamshire
Creed, David	Mod	Hardwick Beast	Buckinghamshire
Davis, Neal	Mini	Symphony for the Devil	Lincolnshire
Davis, Nigel	Mini	Satan's Toy	Essex
Dunn, Gary	PS	Major Tom	Clwyd
Evans, Russell	PS	Never a Nuff	Clwyd
Fitchett, John	SS	Under Pressure	Berkshire
George, Chris	Mod	Avon Lady	Avon
Gooding, Paul	Mod	Golden Bullet	Staffordshire
Hanraads, Dick	PS	Lackham Ballistic	Wiltshire
Hare, Peter	Mod	Torment	Essex
Johnson, Bob	Mod	Renegade	Gloucestershire
Jones, Bill	PS	Smokey Joe	Warwickshire
Jones, Gareth	PS	Overlander	Shropshire
Jones, John	PS	Smokey Joe	Warwickshire
Jones, Philip	PS	Hill Billy	Herefordshire
Lawrence, Mike	Mod	Chariot of Fire II	Somerset
Lay, Chris	SS	Deere Stalker	Bedfordshire
Leamon, Chris	Mini	Porkie	Essex
Leese, Julian	Mod	Short Circuit	Devon
Lewis, Lionel	PS	Overlander	Shropshire
Maddock, Robert	SS	Running Deere	Cheshire
Massey Lads	SS	Perkoil Express	Warwickshire
Middleton, Ashley	Mod	Black Gold	Somerset
Morris, Kevin	PS	Happy Wanderer	Wiltshire
Morris, Neil	PS	Double Trouble	Wiltshire
Pacey, Mark	Mini	Mr Magoo	Northamptonshire
Pacey, Mark	Mod	Hot Pot	Northamptonshire

Parker, Ian	PS	French Connection	Shropshire
Pollard, Alan	PS	Poldark	Northamptonshire
Powell, David	PS	Little Willie	Herefordshire
Prince, Dave	Mod	Just Another Invader	Somerset
Roberts, Stephen	PS	Shropshire Lad	Shropshire
Rosewell, William	Mod	Old Ironsides	Devon
Shepherd, Alan	Mini	Milford Lady	Hampshire
Shirley, Ian	Mod	Knightmare	Warwickshire
Shirley, Joe	Mod	Knightmare	Warwickshire
Shore, David	SS	Lethal Weapon	Cheshire
Simmons, Mike	PS	Hit 'n' Miss	Shropshire
Snell, Jim	Mod	Starlight Express II	Devon
Stone, Martin	TWD	Bounty Hunter	Somerset
Summers, John	Mod	Sleepless Nights	Wiltshire
Traisneau, Peter	PS	Deere Experience	Cambridgeshire
Uphill, Robert	PS	Uphill Struggle	Somerset
Wevell, Guy	Mini	Trevethick's Dream	Cornwall
White, Paul	PS	Deere Experience	Bedford
Whitnell, Mick	Mini	Turbo Charger	Essex
Whittingham, Kevan	Mod	Snoopy	Lancashire
Whittingham, Paul	Mod	Snoopy	Lancashire
Williams, Alan	Mod	Limited Edition	Clwyd
Williams, Paul	SS	Rough Justice	Clwyd

* Mini = 900 kg mini modified; Mod = modified; PS = pro stock; SS = super stock; TWD = two-wheel drive trucks

Pro stock tractors after weighing in—all are lined up close to the track, waiting for the class to start.

Appendix II
BTPA results 1991 & 1992

Competitors are listed in winning order. Only those tractors that scored points have been included. In most instances, additional tractors took part but did not finish high enough to receive points.

In the case of a tie, a coin is usually thrown, or if one competitor has won a title in another weight class, he/she may give the title to the other driver. For example, in 1991, the driver of Just Another Invader, having won the 3400 kg modified, agreed to take second place when he tied with Limited Edition in the 2400 kg modified.

1991 BRITISH CHAMPIONSHIP RESULTS

900 kg Mini Modified

Tractor		Total points
477	Trevethick's Dream	209
509	Stray Cat	206
502	Top Cat	191
484	Porkie	155
463	Mr Magoo	128
519	Satan's Toy	114
456	Hurtmore Horror	111
513	Milford Lady	106
458	Groundhog	102
517	Fat Cat	102
514	Turbocharger	24

2400 kg Modified

Tractor		Total points
75	Limited Edition	117
500	Just Another Invader	117
358	Renegade	92
451	Alley Cat	79
98	Firefox	45
35	Avon Lady	19

3400 kg Pro Stock

Tractor		Total points
116	French Connection	186
373	Major Tom	165
375	Never A Nuff	148
504	Little Willie	146
450	Hit 'n' Miss	144
486	Happy Wanderer	107
515	Overlander	74
80	Smokey Joe	58

361	Poldark	58
512	Lackham Ballistic	46
510	Odds 'n' Ends	43
518	Hill Billy	43
160	Deere Experience Too	40
52	Uphill Struggle	21
453	Red Baron	7

3400 kg Super Stock

Tractor		Total points
350	Running Deere	177
151	JBJ Express	142
378	Perkoil Express	126
160	Deere Stalker	71
80	Smokey Joe	27
19	Under Pressure	24
450	Hit 'n' Miss	21
453	Red Baron	21
516	Leathal Weapon	21

3400 kg Modified

Tractor		Total points
500	Just Another Invader	138
169	Desperate Dan	128
197	Starlight Express II	107
75	Limited Edition	101
511	Hot Pot	59
358	Renegade	49
51	Short Circuit	45
266	Knightmare II	36
36	Avon Lady	20

4400 kg Pro Stock

Tractor		Total points
116	French Connection	162
373	Major Tom	153
450	Hit 'n' Miss	131
486	Happy Wanderer	123
504	Little Willie	120
375	Never A Nuff	89
361	Poldark	51
515	Overlander	50
518	Hill Billy	48
510	Odds 'n' Ends	38
160	Deere Experience Too	37
52	Uphill Struggle	26
453	Red Baron	14
512	Lackham Ballistic	14
80	Smokey Joe	11

4400 kg Super Stock

Class		Total points
350	Running Deere	147
378	Perkoil Express	143
151	JBJ Express	118
450	Hit 'n' Miss	84
515	Overlander	78
61	Deere Experience Too	40
516	Lethal Weapon	37
453	Red Baron	32
116	French Connection	24
19	Under Pressure	22
80	Smokey Joe	19
52	Uphill Struggle	15

4400 kg Modified

Tractor		Total points
169	Desperate Dan	162
500	Just Another Invader	159
7	Snoopy	146
197	Starlight Express II	133
511	Hot Pot	87

353	Chariot of Fire II	63
266	Knightmare II	51
51	Short Circuit	44
454	Chariot of Fire I	21
376	Old Ironsides	15
503	Torment	13
75	Limited Edition	5

5700 kg Modified

Tractor		Total Points
7	Snoopy	144
353	Chariot of Fire II	89
169	Desperate Dan	59
376	Old Ironsides	48
454	Chariot of Fire I	21

1992 BRITISH CHAMPIONSHIP RESULTS

900 kg Mini Modified

Tractor		Total points
458	Groundhog	184
509	Stray Cat	180
519	Satan's Toy	175
502	Top Cat	163
484	Porkie	145
456	Hurtmore Horror	132
463	Mr Magoo	125
513	Milford Lady	106
517	Symphony for the Devil	13

2400 kg Modified

Tractor		Total points
521	Black Gold	109
500	Just Another Invader	84
75	Limited Edition	70
451	Alley Cat	64
358	Renegade	40
35	Avon Lady	24

3400 kg Pro Stock

Tractor		Total points
373	Major Tom	150
116	French Connection	129
450	Hit 'n' Miss	112
504	Little Willie	105
486	Happy Wanderer	99
515	Overlander	67
518	Hill Billy	62
80	Smokey Joe	57
510	Double Trouble	26
375	Never A Nuff	18
512	Lackham Ballistic	18
52	Uphill Struggle	15
462	Shropshire Lad	11
453	Red Baron	6

3400 kg Super Stock

Tractor		Total points
151	JBJ Express	139
350	Running Deere	132
378	Perkoil Express	75
80	Smokey Joe	66
453	Red Baron	38
160	Deere Stalker	27
161	Deere Experience Too	24

3400 kg Modified

Tractor		Total points
500	Just Another Invader	111
197	Starlight Express II	100
169	Desperate Dan	84
511	Hot Pot	76
51	Short Circuit	74
521	Black Gold	67
266	Knightmare II	49
36	Avon Lady	34

4400 kg Pro Stock

Tractor		Total points
373	Major Tom	118.5
450	Hit 'n' Miss	106.5
116	French Connection	102.5
486	Happy Wanderer	99.5
515	Overlander	91.5
504	Little Willie	88.5
518	Hill Billy	56.5
80	Smokey Joe	45.5
375	Never A Nuff	44
510	Double Trouble	26.5
512	Lackham Ballistic	24.5
52	Uphill Struggle	22
453	Red Baron	11.5
462	Shropshire Lad	11.5
160	Deere Experience Too	6

4400 kg Super Stock

Class		Total points
350	Running Deere	103
450	Hit 'n' Miss	86
151	JBJ Express	79
515	Overlander	78
116	French Connection	61
80	Smokey Joe	38
378	Perkoil Express	24

4400 kg Modified

Tractor		Total points
169	Desperate Dan	125.5
7	Snoopy	118.5
197	Starlight Express II	104.5
500	Just Another Invader	86.5
521	Black Gold	76.5
511	Hot Pot	72
266	Knightmare II	53
353	Chariot of Fire II	38.5
51	Short Circuit	33.5
376	Old Ironsides	27.5
520	Sleepless Nights	14.5

5700 kg Modified

Tractor		Total points
7	Snoopy	110.5
353	Chariot of Fire II	77.5
511	Hot Pot	69
376	Old Ironsides	46
169	Desperate Dan	27

Index

Italicised numbers refer to illustrations

FARMING PRESS BOOKS & VIDEOS

Below is a sample of the wide range of agricultural and veterinary books and videos published by Farming Press. For more information or for a free illustrated catalogue please contact:

**Farming Press Books & Videos, Wharfedale Road
Ipswich IP1 4LG, United Kingdom
Telephone (0473) 241122   Fax (0473) 240501**

VHS COLOUR VIDEOS

Fordson: the story of a tractor
TOLD BY BOB SYMES

This features the five main Fordson models from 1917 to the 1950s. It combines archive material with new film.

The Massey-Ferguson Story
MICHAEL WILLIAMS

Michael Williams takes us from the early days of Wallis and the General Purpose tractor right up to modern high-spec models.

BOOKS

Tractors Since 1889   MICHAEL WILLIAMS

An overview of the main developments in farm tractors from their stationary engine origins to the potential for satellite naviga-tion. Illustrated.

Tractors: how they work and what they do   MICHAEL WILLIAMS

For younger readers, a highly illustrated account of tractor principles and develop-ment, looking also at larger American and Australian models.

Ford and Fordson Tractors

Massey-Ferguson Tractors
MICHAEL WILLIAMS

Two heavily illustrated guides to the models which made these leading com-panies great.

Farm Workshop   BRIAN BELL

Describes the requirements of the farm workshop and illustrates the uses of the necessary tools and equipment.

Farm Welding   ANDREW PEARCE

Fully illustrated guide to stick welding, gas welding and cutting, MIG/MAG techniques, soldering and basic blacksmithing.

Farming Press Books is part of the Morgan-Grampian Farming Press Group, which also publishes a range of farming magazines: *Arable Farming, Dairy Farmer, Farming News, Pig Farming, What's New in Farming.* For a specimen copy of any of these please contact the address above.